Award-Winning Quilts

Book II

Judy Florence

Cover Design: Ann Eastburn
Interior Layout: Anthony Jacobson

Photographs: Jim Christoffersen

Library of Congress Catalog
Card Number 85-051347

ISBN 0-87069-466-9

Copyright ©1986
Judy Florence

All rights reserved. No part of this publication may be reproduced, stored in a retrieval system, or transmitted in any form or by any means, electronic, mechanical, photocopying, recording or otherwise, without prior permission of the copyright owner or the publisher.

10 9 8 7 6 5 4 3 2 1

Published by

Wallace-Homestead Book Company
580 Waters Edge
Lombard, Illinois 60148

To my husband, Dick.

Contents

Introduction	5
How To Use This Book	6
1 Lilies of the Field	7
2 Computer Kaleidoscope	15
3 A Little Something to Brighten Your Day	23
4 Autumn	29
5 Computer Kaleidoscope II	41
6 Guardian Angel	49
Appendix A: How To Make Narrow Bias Strips for Appliqué	56
Appendix B: More Ideas for Creating Your Own Quilting Designs	58
Bibliography	62
About the Author	63
Templates	64

Introduction

After several years of quilting within the confines of traditional patterns and block-by-block construction, I finally reached what I call the "breaking-out-of-the-block" stage. Familiar patterns and ordinary settings became less appealing. I longed to branch into designs and layouts with more variety. *Award-Winning Quilts, Book II* reflects this transitional phase of my quiltmaking career.

The patterns and techniques of my first book, *Award-Winning Quilts and How To Make Them* are expanded in this second book. Here you will find more challenging patterns, more original quilting designs, and more non-traditional construction methods. Strip-piecing, medallion-style patterns, modified whole-cloth quilts, and computer-generated designs are all part of this book.

Although several of the patterns may be classified as challenging, there remains a broad range of difficulty levels. Experienced quilters might try the intricate and detailed Guardian Angel or Lilies of the Field. Quilters with less experience might begin with the Autumn wall quilt or the Spectrum quilt of many colors.

Each pattern reflects an experiment with an idea or challenge that was new to me. In Lilies of the Field, a striped border fabric is incorporated into a medallion setting. My objective was to experiment with the layout of a directional fabric throughout blocks and borders of varied sizes and widths. I found that the placement of tiny squares, trapezoids, and triangles provided an array of options: Should the stripes go up and down? Across the medallion? Against the borders? Radiating from the center?

A longing to work in the spectrum colors led to A Little Something to Brighten Your Day. Transforming the spacious spectrum panels into "quiltedness" resulted in fourteen original quilting designs.

When I became aware of the challenges and possibilities of computer design, another segment of the quilt world was opened to me. The graphics, colors, and shape variations immediately caught my interest. The hours of pleasure in programming and "playing" at the video monitor are reflected in the Computer Kaleidoscope patterns.

How could I convert a home computer design into fabric? How could I transform a snapshot of a chapel window into a quilt? How could I preserve the message of compassion expressed by an angel and a child? Each of these questions led to another quilt pattern.

The resulting assortment will appeal to both traditional and innovative quilters. The patterns allow room for personal expression and adaptation. Whether you call yourself a novice or master quilter, or something in between, there is a design or an idea that you can use or adapt. In combination with my first book, *Book II* offers a wide range of techniques, styles, and designs.

Page through the book and make your selections. Then enjoy your quilting!

How To Use This Book

The patterns and quilt designs in this book are arranged in a seasonal format, from spring to winter, beginning with Lilies of the Field and concluding with Guardian Angel. Two wall hangings (crib-size quilts) and four bed-size quilts are included. Each chapter includes a commentary, directions, and patterns.

The commentary gives the story behind the quilt. It may tell where the idea came from or why the quilt was made. It may also include comments on how to convert the pattern to other sizes, colors, and fabric options, and ways to give the pattern your personal touch. The commentary may also suggest the pleasures and pitfalls each quilt involves.

The directions include complete instructions and diagrams, including the finished size, a list of required fabric and supplies, and step-by-step guidelines for cutting, assembly, quilting, and finishing.

The patterns are full size and include more than twenty-five original quilting designs.

The directions assume a general knowledge of the basics of piecing and appliqué. For specific help on precision cutting and piecing, preparing the layers for quilting, and binding a quilt, refer to the Appendix section of my first book, *Award-Winning Quilts*. Other elementary patterns are also given in that book.

Special instructional materials, advice, and how-to's that pertain to several of the quilts are given in this book's Appendix section. Look there for tips on how to make narrow bias strips for appliqué and how to create your own quilting designs.

For general information on quiltmaking techniques, additional pattern ideas, and sources of inspiration, nostalgia or history, see the recommended references in the Bibliography.

1
Lilies of the Field

Many quilters are attracted to the Lilies pattern because it includes the best of both worlds — piecing and appliqué — without an over-abundance of either. In addition, the medallion setting is a refreshing alternative to traditional block-to-block setting.

Lilies is not a large quilt. It measures 64" square, which is a nice coverlet size. Its visual impact and interest also make it ideal for a wall hanging. The skill level is of medium difficulty — probably not for beginners, but appropriate for anyone who has had some quiltmaking experience.

Lilies incorporates a striped calico print fabric throughout the quilt design. All the other fabrics are solid colors found within the print. They include dark blue, light blue, medium green, dark green, yellow, and orange.

The traditional North Carolina Lily pattern is somewhat altered. The bottom of the flower is enlarged and subdivided into nine triangles that serve as a base or pot for the lilies. The four pots form a background square for the central medallion.

Four traditional honeybee squares placed adjacent to one another comprise the central medallion. The wings and bodies of the bees are appliquéd and stuffed slightly to give a realistic effect.

One of the most enjoyable parts of planning this quilt was the creation of quilting designs for the light blue and dark blue background areas. These were made by experimenting with the layout of two of the appliqué shapes — the leaf of the lily and the body of the bee. Both of these "teardrop" shapes lend themselves well to endless design possibilities.

Through the process of superimposing these shapes, tracing, and selective erasing, you, too, can make original and appropriate designs. Start with cardboard templates of the teardrop shapes, paper, and a pencil with a good eraser. The three original quilting motifs used in Lilies are included in the instructional section. See Appendix B for more ideas.

Preparing bias strips for the flower stems can be simplified and streamlined. Custom-made bias from matching fabric is usually sturdier and visually more acceptable than commercial bias. (See Appendix A.) Strips such as these can be used for stems, vines, basket handles, Celtic work, stained glass, and other appliqué work.

The design variations for the Lilies quilt are endless. A different color theme, a different pattern in place of the North Carolina lily or the honeybee, or your own special quilt design will give this project a personal touch.

Directions

Finished Size: 64" square.

Fabric and other materials. *Note:* Fabrics should be 44"/45" wide in cotton or cotton/polyester blend.

Print stripe....2 yards

Dark blue....2 yards
  (set aside 1 yard for binding)

Light blue....1 yard

Dark green....¼ yard

Medium green....¼ yard

Yellow....1¾ yards

Orange....½ yard

Backing....4 yards
  (good-quality unbleached muslin)

Batting....72" by 90"
  (bonded polyester)

Matching sewing thread, scissors, lightweight cardboard for templates, ruler, quilting needles, two spools of light blue quilting thread, thimble, soap chips, washable marking pencils, pins, iron, and hoop or frame for quilting.

Color Key

P   = Print

DB = Dark Blue

LB = Light Blue

DG = Dark Green

MG = Medium Green

Y   = Yellow

O   = Orange

Cutting

Note: This quilt is composed of four honeybee blocks and eight North Carolina Lily blocks, with large squares, triangles, trapezoids, and borders to complete the medallion setting.

There are eighteen pattern pieces coded L-1 through L-18 (L stands for Lilies). Note that all seam allowances are ¼" and must be added to the pattern pieces. The honeybee blocks use templates L-1, L-2, L-3, L-4, and L-5. The North Carolina Lily blocks use templates L-6 through and including L-14. Patterns L-15 through L-18 are for the large triangles, etc., that complete the medallion. Please note and observe the suggested grain-line arrows on all pieces. Cut the following pattern pieces.

L- 1: Cut four orange, sixteen print, and sixteen dark blue (total of thirty-six.)

L- 2: Cut sixteen light blue

L- 3: Cut sixteen light blue

L- 4: Cut thirty-two yellow

L- 5: Cut sixteen orange

L- 6: Cut eight light blue (place on fold)

L- 7: Cut sixteen light blue

L- 8: Cut forty-eight yellow and forty-eight orange (total of ninety-six)

L-9: Cut forty-eight light blue

L-10: Cut twenty-four light blue

L-11: Cut twenty-four medium green

L-12: Cut twenty-four dark green

L-13: Cut sixteen medium green

L-14: Cut forty-eight dark blue and twenty-four orange (total of seventy-two)

L-15: Cut twenty dark blue (⅛ of a 12¾″ square)

L-16: Cut four dark blue (¼ of a 12¾″ square)

L-17: Cut twelve print (6⅜″ square)

L-18: Cut four print (place on fold)

Cut the following borders (seam allowances included).

Yellow: Cut four strips, each 1½″ by 57½″

Print: Cut four panels, each 4″ by 64½″

Assembly

Make four honeybee blocks as in Diagram 1. Join the center squares (pattern L-1) in a nine-patch fashion. Attach a rectangle (L-3) on two opposite sides. Join the other rectangles (L-3) between two (L-2) squares. Repeat. Attach these to the other sides of the nine-patch unit. Turn under ¼″ on the edges of the body (L-5) and wings (L-4) for all bees. Appliqué the wings and bodies to the pieced block. Join the four honeybee blocks for the center of the quilt as in Diagram 2.

Diagram 1

Honeybee	Honeybee
Honeybee	Honeybee

Diagram 2

Make eight Lily blocks as in Diagram 3. Join four diamonds (L-8). Add the corner square (L-10) and two triangles (L-9). Add the triangle base (L-11). Repeat twice to make three flower units. Join nine triangles (L-14) to form the larger triangular base for the block. Position three stems (L-12) and two leaves (L-13), with raw edges turned under, onto the background (L-6). Applique in place. Attach the pieced triangular base. Sew a square (L-7) between two pieced flowers. Join another square (L-7) to the remaining flower, then to the appliquéd portion. Join the two sections to complete the block.

To make Unit A, join a dark blue triangle (L-15) to the 9″ side of the large trapezoid (L-18). See Diagram 4. Make four of these. Attach Unit "A" to each of the four sides of the honeybee center. See Diagram 5.

To make Unit B, join the Lily blocks in pairs, with the pieced triangle bases together as in Diagram 6. Make four of these.

To make Unit C, join two large print squares (L-17). Attach a large dark blue triangle (L-16) to one long side and small triangles (L-15) to each end, as shown in Diagram 7. Make four of these units. Attach a Unit C to each pair of Lily blocks (Unit B) as shown in Diagram 8. Make four.

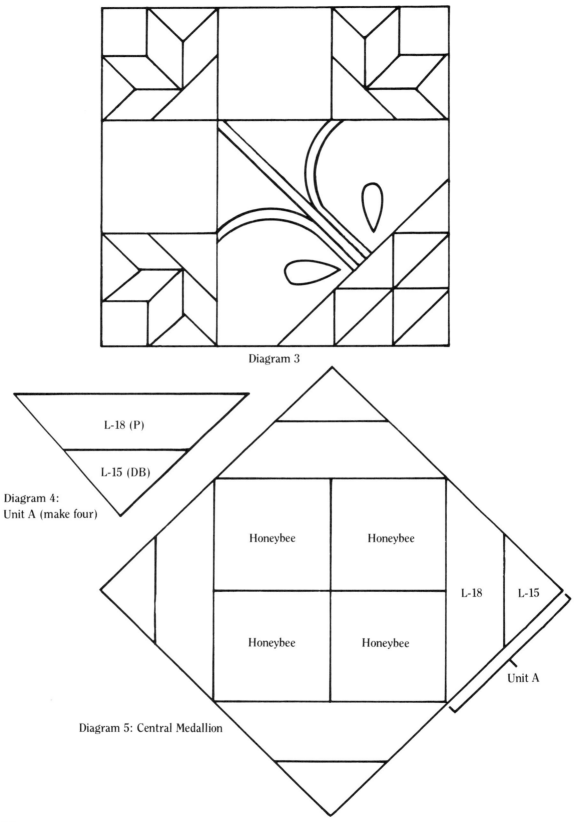

Diagram 3

Diagram 4: Unit A (make four)

Diagram 5: Central Medallion

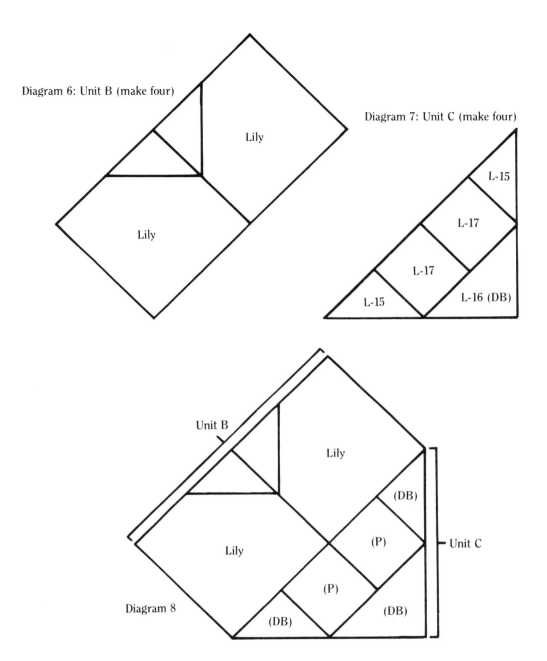

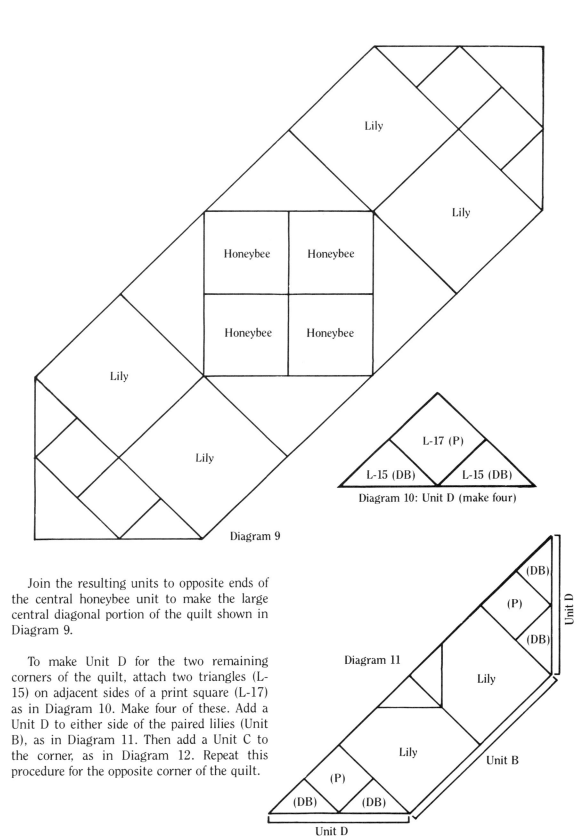

Diagram 9

Diagram 10: Unit D (make four)

Diagram 11

Join the resulting units to opposite ends of the central honeybee unit to make the large central diagonal portion of the quilt shown in Diagram 9.

To make Unit D for the two remaining corners of the quilt, attach two triangles (L-15) on adjacent sides of a print square (L-17) as in Diagram 10. Make four of these. Add a Unit D to either side of the paired lilies (Unit B), as in Diagram 11. Then add a Unit C to the corner, as in Diagram 12. Repeat this procedure for the opposite corner of the quilt.

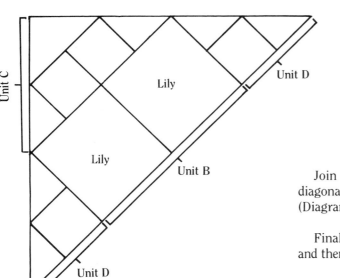

Diagram 12

Join these two corner units to the central diagonal honeybee unit to complete the top (Diagram 13).

Finally, attach the narrow yellow borders and then the wide print borders.

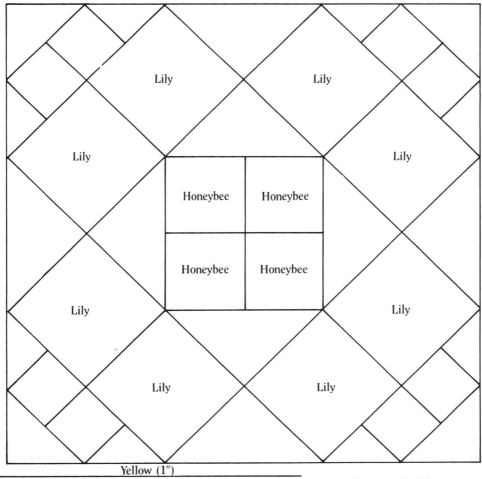

Diagram 13: Lilies Layout

Quilting

Sandwich the quilt back, batting, and top together. Baste through all layers. Mount in a frame or hoop. Using light blue thread, quilt around all shapes and blocks close to the seams. Use the small square floral quilting design in the solid light blue areas of the lily squares (L-7). Mark the small triangular quilting design in the medium-sized blue triangles (L-15) and the larger triangular design in the large dark blue triangles (L-16). Quilt straight lines along the stripes of the printed fabric (trapezoids, large squares, and wide borders). Quilt two parallel lines along the yellow border. Stitch ¼" from the edges on the diamonds of the flower petals (L-8), the base of the flowers (L-11), the orange triangles (L-14), the stems, and the leaves.

Finishing

Remove the basting. Make bias binding from the one-yard piece of dark blue fabric and attach it to the quilt front. Turn it to the back and blindstitch it in place.

2
Computer Kaleidoscope I

Several years ago I became aware of the possibility of designing quilts on a home computer. Immediately my interest in computers skyrocketed and a computer sounded like a sensible, justifiable investment. If I could experiment with quilt designs, our family needed a home computer.

Most of my early computer design experiments were with multicolored rectangular patterns, such as Computer Kaleidoscope. After I had mastered the basics (the very basics, mind you, and not much more), I began to write and adapt programs for various geometric patterns. I learned to control variables such as the segment size and shape, the number of colors, and the layout. This resulted in many hours of visual pleasure, as I watched patterns form on the screen by the dozens, hundreds, and thousands. I could study the designs, select my favorites, and dream of the infinite number of quilts that could be made.

When I finally selected and studied a design that I wanted to execute in fabric, I used the television hand controls (brightness, contrast, color, and tint) to visualize the color possibilities. I could remove all color and imagine a quilt in black, white, and grays. I could increase the brightness to bring an iridescence to the pattern. A slight variation with the color control would change the design from soft natural, peach, cyan, and ivory to brighter yellow, pink, lavender, and green, with all degrees of change in between.

Computer Kaleidoscope was my first quilt based on a design generated on my home computer. After I had sketched the design from the screen, I studied my swatch samples and selected a combination of natural tones much as they appeared on my color monitor. I chose black and cyan borders and binding to accentuate the central kaleidoscopic design.

Since one of my biggest problems was designing the quilt from a small screen that measures only 8" x 11", I concentrated next on devising a program that would determine what size to make the pieces and how much fabric to order. I made layouts for standard quilt sizes (wall, twin, double, and queen) and wrote a program that would tell me how much fabric to buy. I let the computer do the work. After obtaining yardage requirements for a double bed (Computer Kaleidoscope measures 84" x 96"), I selected and ordered fabric through a mail-order firm.

The assembly of C.K. is quite elementary. Although there are several shapes in the design, it is not necessary to make any templates or patterns. Instead, all the fabrics are cut in strips of varying widths, then they are pieced together and re-cut into panel designs. All the piecing can be done by machine. The cutting can be done with a rotary cutter, mat, and straightedge or a good-quality fabric scissors. The entire top could be assembled in a couple of days. After you've become familiar with this technique, you will find it easy and efficient.

Beyond the first pleasure of designing on a computer came the enjoyment of experimenting with quilting lines across the surface. I would mark projecting lines, angles, pyramids, and crisscrossings until I had something that suited me. I changed my mind several times along the way and removed many marked and quilted lines. I made a vow to give up in-the-ditch quilting on this work, only to find that this was the very pattern on which in-the-ditch had its best delineation effect. I ditch-stitched around all the fabric segments and settled on an overall quilted gridwork of elongated X's, angular lines radiating from the center sides, top, and bottom, and parallel diagonal lines on the borders.

Adaptability to various bed sizes and a choice of several symmetrical/asymmetrical layouts are two of the flexible features of computer designs.

You don't need a computer, or even computer knowledge and experience to try this design. Complete directions and diagrams for the layout and construction of Computer Kaleidoscope are given. Just select your favorite range of colors and see what you can create.

Directions

Finished Size: 84" x 96".

Fabric and Other Materials. *Note:* Fabrics should be 44"/45" wide in cotton or cotton/polyester blends.

Natural....2½ yards

Blue....1½ yards

Cyan....3¾ yards
  (This amount includes enough for borders and binding.)

Spice....1 yard

Teal....½ yard

Ivory....½ yard

Black....3 yards
  (for borders)

Backing....6 yards (good-quality unbleached muslin or natural color fabric)

Batting....90" x 108"
  (bonded polyester)

Sewing thread to match fabrics, two spools of black quilting thread, thread for basting, iron, scissors, rustproof pins, sharp lead pencils, quilting needles, thimble, 18" ruler or 22" straightedge, soap chips or washable dressmaker pencils, and quilting hoop or frame.

Color Key

N = Natural

B = Blue

C = Cyan

S = Spice

T = Teal

I = Ivory

Cutting

Computer Kaleidoscope is cut and assembled using quick-cutting and machine-piecing techniques. There are no templates. All cutting is done in strips and rows. A rotary cutter and mat is especially appropriate for this pattern. All seams are ¼". The quilt is assembled in rows, rather than blocks. The top is assembled in quarter sections, which in turn are joined to complete the design. Please read through all instructions and diagrams before cutting any fabrics.

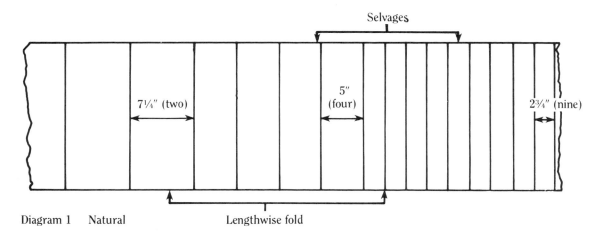

Diagram 1   Natural

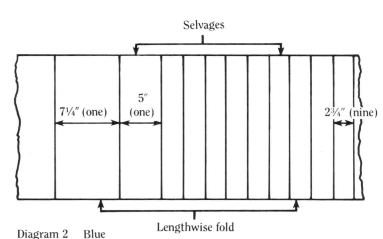

Diagram 2   Blue

Assembly

Wash, dry, and press all fabrics.

Begin with the natural color fabric (2½ yards). Fold it in half lengthwise, right sides together, and pin to secure it. (If you are using solid color fabrics, there is no right or wrong side of the fabric, for all practical purposes.) With a long straightedge and a soap chip or washable pencil, mark nine narrow strips, each 2¾" wide, across the folded fabric, as in Diagram 1*. (Marked units will be about 22" long, depending on the exact width of your folded fabric.) Next mark four medium strips, each 5" wide, on the folded fabric. Last, mark two wide strips, each 7¼". Note that a ¼" seam allowance is included on all strip measurements.

Note: If you use a long straightedge with width markings and a rotary cutter, you may simply cut the strips at the proper intervals and omit the marking step. Cut all the strips on the marked lines. Then cut along the fold at the end of the strips.

Mark and cut the remaining five fabrics according to Diagrams 2 through 6. Remember to cut across the folded end as well. For cyan fabric only, cut one additional strip 16¼" x 22" from a single layer of fabric only.

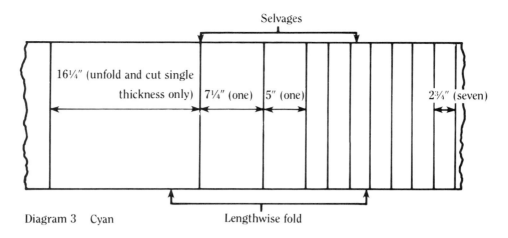

Diagram 3 Cyan

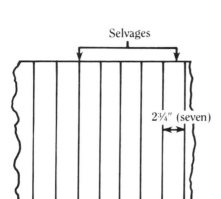

Diagram 4
Spice

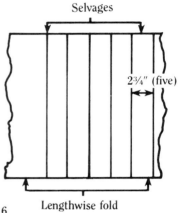

Diagram 6
Ivory

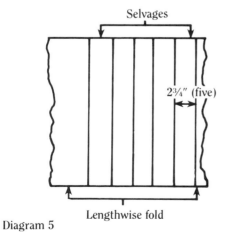

Diagram 5
Teal

Begin with Row 1 and gather the required strips from top to bottom (Row 1 will have twelve strips). See Diagrams 7 and 8. Mark this pile of strips with a label "Row 1" and set aside. Likewise, gather the strips for the remaining seven rows (Diagram 7) and label them.

Row 1: twelve strips
Row 2: sixteen strips
Row 3: ten strips
Row 4: fifteen strips
Row 5: twelve strips
Row 6: twelve strips
Row 7: twelve strips
Row 8: ten strips

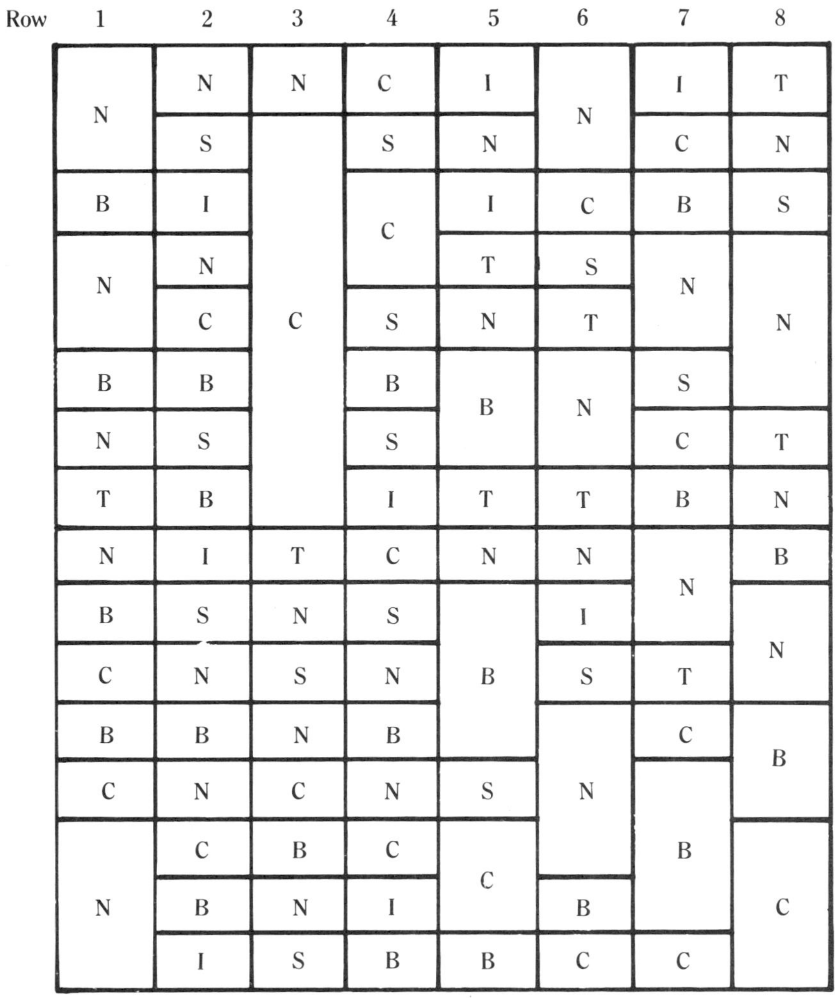

Row	1	2	3	4	5	6	7	8
	N	N	N	C	I	N	I	T
	N	S		S	N	N	C	N
	B	I		C	I	C	B	S
	N	N	C	C	T	S	N	N
	N	C	C	S	N	T	N	N
	B	B		B	B	N	S	N
	N	S		S	B	N	C	T
	T	B		I	T	T	B	N
	N	I	T	C	N	N	N	B
	B	S	N	S	N	I	N	N
	C	N	S	N	B	S	T	N
	B	B	N	B	B	N	C	B
	C	N	C	N	S	N	C	B
	N	C	B	C	C	B	B	C
	N	B	N	I	C	B	B	C
	N	I	S	B	B	C	C	C

Color Key N = Natural B = Blue C = Cyan S = Spice T = Teal I = Ivory

Diagram 7: One-fourth of quilt top

Gathering and labeling the strips for each row will assure that you have the correct number and color of strips before proceeding with assembly. If there is any discrepancy at this point, cut any additional required pieces. There will be a few extra cut strips (probably six) to add to your scrap bag.

With right sides together, pin the long sides of the strips of Row 1, as in Diagram 8. One end of each strip should be made flush with the next. (They will be uneven at the other end.) Join in ¼" seams. Set Row 1 aside. Likewise, join the strips of the remaining seven rows. Press the seams of all odd-numbered rows up and the seams of all even-numbered rows down.

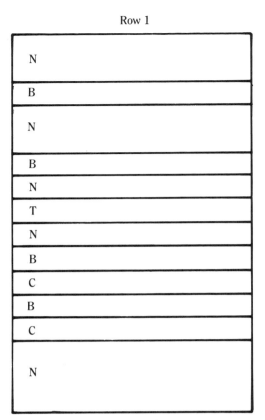

Diagram 8

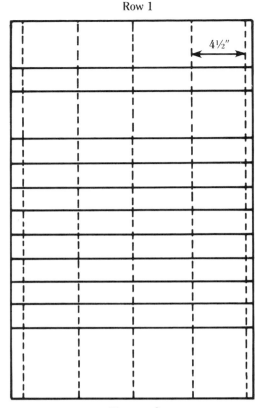

Diagram 9

Lay the assembled Row 1 on a flat surface or cutting mat with the wrong side up. With a straightedge, mark a line along the one side where the edges are flush. Mark four more lines at 4½" intervals, resulting in four columns (see Diagram 9).

Carefully cut along the marked lines. There will be some waste at the other side. Label these four strips "Row 1" and set aside. Repeat the marking and cutting for the remaining seven rows. For Row 8, only two of the cut columns will be used. Put the other two in the scrap pile.

Assemble one quarter-section of the quilt by joining Row 1 to Row 2, etc., through Row 8 (see Diagram 7). Repeat for another quarter-section of the quilt.

Join the remaining two quarter-sections in reverse order, Row 7 through Row 1, with Row 8 omitted entirely. Press all seams to one side. Join the four quarter sections to complete the central design (about 60" x 72") as in Diagram 10.

Cut the following borders. Measurements include allowances for seams and mitering.

Black: Cut two 3½" x 78½"
       Cut two 3½" x 66½"
       Cut two 5½" x 96½"
       Cut two 5½" x 84½"
Cyan: Cut two 4½" x 86½"
       Cut two 4½" x 74½"

Add the borders to the central design. Begin with the 3½" black border, then the 4½" cyan border, and end with the 5½" black border. Miter all corners.

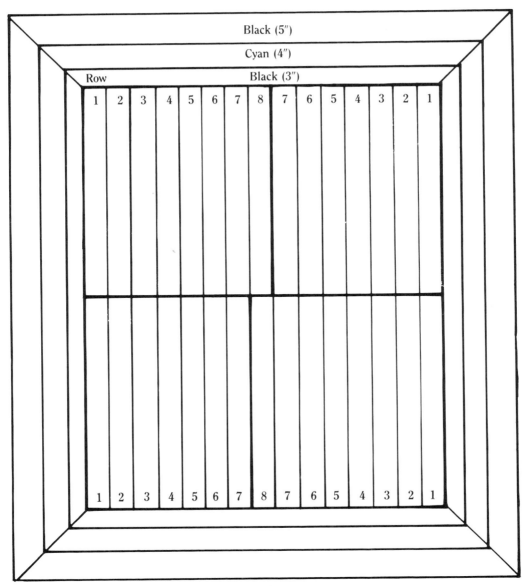

Diagram 10

Cut two pieces from the backing fabric, each about 3 yards long. Split one piece in half lengthwise. Use the uncut piece as the center panel and sew a split width to each side of it. Press seams toward the outside.

Make a "sandwich" of the backing, batting, and pieced top. Baste the three layers together, working from the center to the outside. Place in a hoop or frame and quilt with black quilting thread. Quilt along all seam lines on the side opposite the pressed seam allowances. Quilt an elongated X (as illustrated in Diagram 11) in most teal and spice segments and in most double and triple segments of all the other colors. Quilt two X's in the large cyan areas in each corner. Quilt additional lines as illustrated in Diagram 11. Quilt parallel diagonal lines on the borders.

Make bias binding from the remaining cyan fabric and attach it to the quilt.

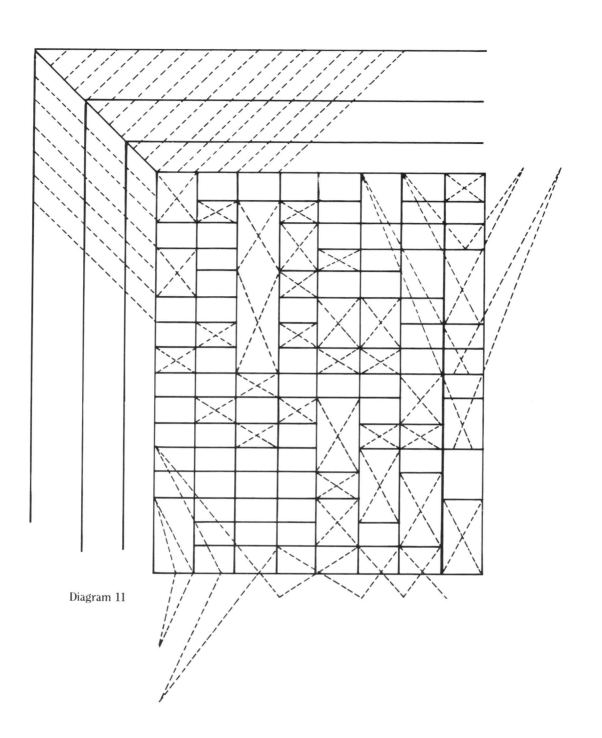

Diagram 11

3
A Little Something to Brighten Your Day

One of the hazards in quiltmaking is color fatigue — growing weary of the predominant colors while working on a project for a long time. After several days, weeks, or months on a project, quilters are often relieved to move on to another color scheme. As I move into the next quilt project, I find myself shifting from browns and beiges to bright blues and yellows, back to soft natural tones, then on to other brighter colors.

The beauty of Spectrum lies in its variety of colors. All colors of the rainbow are included — red, orange, yellow, green, blue, indigo, and violet. The movement from one color panel to the next makes the piecing and quilting processes enjoyable.

I have used fourteen fabrics in Spectrum, including two each of seven colors. If you have a limited supply or access to solid colors, the quilt can be adapted to seven fabrics, each repeated in the center panels. For that matter, you may use any of your favorite color combinations. Even fine prints work well in this design.

Spectrum is easy to assemble. There are no templates and no patterns to cut. The center panels are large and the entire top can be pieced efficiently on the sewing machine. Preassembled strips are used in the borders and binding.

Here is a good opportunity to perfect your quilting skills, as you will spend most of your time quilting rather than piecing and doing applique. The large center panels allow room to express your creativity in quilt designs. The directions include seven selected designs, and you can add some of your own.

Spectrum is easily converted to a larger size by increasing the border widths. It can also be decreased to wall-hanging size by eliminating the pieced border and the wide outer black border.

All of the panel quilting designs are original. Some have a traditional look, and others are more contemporary. Several are the result of inspirations from authentic American Indian designs on pottery, basketry, and quillwork. Others are by-products of my attempts to make tessellation (mosaic) patterns. Still others are the result of playful experiments with a pencil, a ruler, and an eraser on a long piece of paper. The process of creating a quilt pattern and executing it on fabric is gratifying. You can experience this same satisfaction by making your own special designs that reflect your personal interests.

The visual impact of the spectrum colors depends on the black background. Black multiplies the brightness and vitality of the colored panels and pieced border. Any other background color will lessen the impact and perhaps create a washed-out effect.

I have titled this quilt A Little Something to Brighten Your Day. That is what it did for me. I did the quilting on Spectrum in rather dismal weather, with rainy, foggy, overcast gray days. Each time I approached the frame to continue the quilting, I felt a surge of warmth and brightness from the colorful layout. It literally did brighten several of my days. I hope it will brighten yours, too.

Directions

Finished Size. 65" x 87½"

Fabric and Other Materials. *Note:* Fabrics should be 44"/45" 100 percent cotton.

One-half yard each of fourteen colors (select two each of the seven colors of the spectrum — red, orange, yellow, green, blue, indigo, and violet). For variation, you may select and buy one yard each of seven colors and repeat each color in the quilt top.

Black for borders....2½ yards

Backing....5 yards
   (good-quality unbleached muslin)

Batting....72" x 90"
   (bonded polyester)

Two spools of regular sewing thread in a medium neutral color, two spools of natural color quilting thread, fabric scissors or a rotary cutter and mat, large cutting surface area, sewing machine, yardstick or long straightedge, large plastic right triangle, pencil, washable fabric markers or soap chips, quilting needles, thimble, pins, quilting frame or hoop, tape measure, iron, and thread for basting.

Cutting and Assembly

This quilt can be machine-pieced quickly and efficiently. The colored border and binding are strip-pieced. The center is assembled first and then the borders are added, with allowances for mitering. The quilt is then hand-quilted and bound. All seams are ¼". All fabrics should be washed, dried, and pressed before cutting. Carefully read through all directions and diagrams. This is especially important. There is some error allowance in yardage amounts, but there is no room for gross errors.

Color Key

R = Red

O = Orange

Y = Yellow

G = Green

B = Blue

I = Indigo

V = Violet

Begin with one of the fourteen colors and cut a strip 5" x 41" (seam allowances included). This strip will be along the crosswise of the ½ yard fabric piece. Make a similar strip (5" x 41") from each of the fourteen colors. If you are using a good-quality fabric scissors, you may pin and cut several layers of fabric at once. If you are using a rotary cutter and mat, you may also cut several layers at once.

Lay the fourteen strips in the order of the spectrum (red, orange, yellow, green, blue, indigo, violet). With right sides together, sew along the long sides in ¼" seams. The assembled center unit should measure 41" x 63½", including the seams. See Diagram 1.

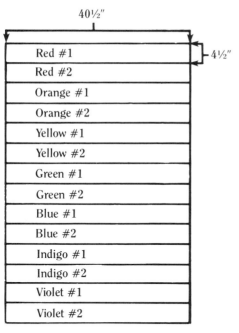

Diagram 1

Black borders. For the narrow inner borders, cut two strips 2¾" x 47" and two strips 2¾" x 70" (allowances for seams and miters included). For the wide outer black borders, cut two strips 6" by 67" and two strips 6" by 90" (allowances for seams and miters included). Attach the narrow black borders (2¼") to the center panel of colors. See Diagram 4. Miter the corners. Set the outer wide (6") borders aside.

Diagonal-strip color borders. From each of the fourteen colors, cut four crosswise strips measuring 2⅛" wide and as long as possible on the crosswise width of the fabric (fabrics will vary from 41" to 45" wide). For more efficient cutting, you may mark the four strips on one fabric and pin several other colors underneath to cut at the same time.

Assembly of diagonal-strip border. Lay the 2⅛" strips on a large, flat surface. Place them in order, with the end of each strip staggered (in a stairstep fashion) about 1½" to the right of the strip below. See Diagram 2. Pin and join all fourteen strips in ¼" seams. Press all seams in one direction. Set the unit aside and repeat for the other three sets of colored strips.

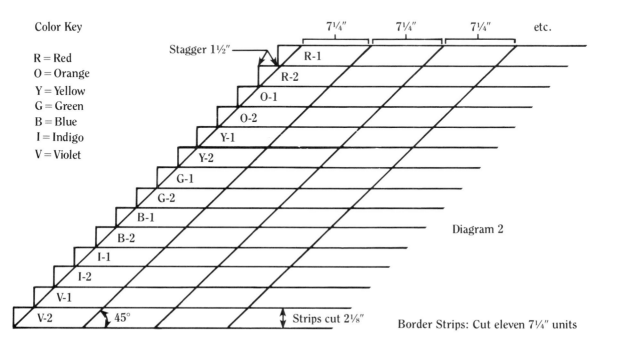

Border Strips: Cut eleven 7¼" units

Diagram 2

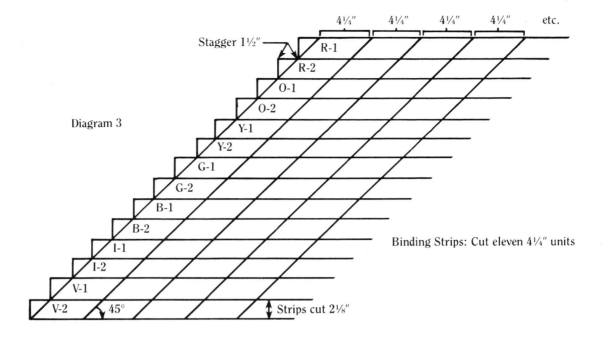

Diagram 3

Binding Strips: Cut eleven 4¼" units

Cutting diagonal strips. With a long straightedge and a large right triangle (45- and 90-degree angles), mark diagonal strips at 7¼" horizontal intervals and at 45-degree angles. See Diagram 2. Use of a large triangle or the diagonal markings on a cutting board will help ensure accuracy. Cut a total of eleven 7¼" interval strips.

Note: It is important to distinguish between the interval width and the resulting cut width of the diagonal strips. They are marked at a 7¼" horizontal interval. When cut, the strips will measure 4½" wide from raw edge to raw edge.

For binding (to be attached after all quilting is completed), mark and cut diagonal strips at 4¼" intervals. Cut a total of eleven of the narrow diagonal strips. Set these aside for binding. See Diagram 3.

Note: Binding strips are marked at a 4¼" horizontal interval. When cut, they will measure 3" wide from raw edge to raw edge.

Assembly of diagonal border strips. Join the wide border strips into four continuous units long enough for the sides and ends. Make the units long enough to allow for natural miters at the corners. You may have to take apart and rejoin a few short seams between the colors. Pin these to the quilt center, one side at a time, and sew in a ¼" seam. Miter the corners as shown in Diagram 4.

Attach the outer 6" wide black borders in ¼" seams with mitered corners, as shown in Diagram 4.

From the 5-yard unbleached muslin piece, cut two pieces each about 2½" yards long for the backing. Leave one piece uncut. Cut two 15" wide strips from the other piece and attach them to either side of the uncut panel, resulting in one wide central panel with two narrow side panels. Use ¼" seams, press the seams toward the outside.

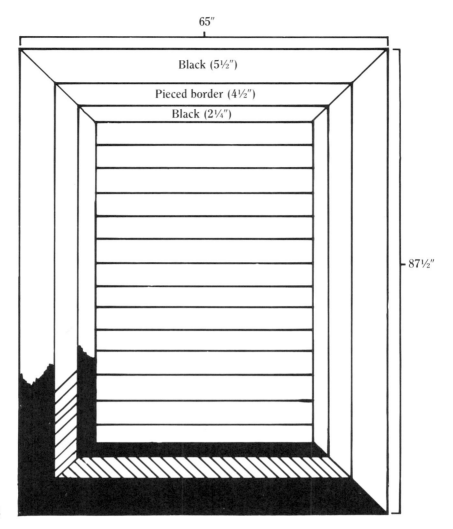

Diagram 4

Make a "sandwich" of the backing, batting, and pieced quilt top. Baste or pin the three layers together, working outward from the center. Place in a frame or hoop and quilt with natural colored quilting thread. The diagonal quilting lines in the borders may be marked with masking tape, triangle and soap chip, or washable fabric marker. See Diagram 5. Selected quilting designs in the central panels may also be done as you go, using pins to locate points for all straight lines and a cardboard template for any curved designs. The same quilting design may be repeated in all the center panels. You may choose seven designs, repeating each twice, or you may add creations of your own for fourteen different designs.

Make 3" wide bias binding by assembling the narrow diagonal strips into one continuous bias strip to total about 325" in length. Fold the binding in half, wrong sides together, and attach it to the quilt front, placing raw edges even with the edge of the quilt front. Stitch in a ¼" seam through all layers. Turn the binding to the quilt back and slip-stitch it in place.

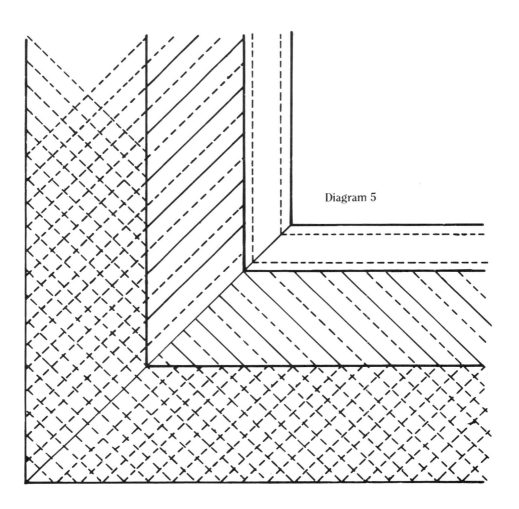

Diagram 5

4

Autumn

With the end of summer vacations, back-to-school for the children, and the return of cooler days and nights, many quilters experience their strongest urge to get back to quilting. The Autumn wall quilt would make a timely kickoff for the quilting season. It's something special for fall.

The quilted designs that cover the Autumn panels are reminiscent of harvest time and Halloween — a sheaf of wheat, an ear of corn, acorns, an oak leaf, an apple, a jack-o'-lantern, and a maple leaf. You could include other ideas, such as a ghost or goblin, a pheasant or turkey, a cornucopia or chrysanthemum.

A blend of brown, tan, peach, rust, and golden hues is used on the panels of this modified whole-cloth top. The panels and borders can be cut and assembled in a short time, especially if you use a rotary cutter, mat, and straightedge. The three border fabrics may be stacked and cut simultaneously. The seven center panels may be cut in the same manner. Assembly is by machine, with all straight seams. No intricate piecing is required.

The Autumn quilt is appropriate for both beginning and experienced quilters. The directions are easy to follow, and there is ample room for personal expression by mixing some prints with the solids, increasing the color range, or making your own quilting designs.

It is possible that you will put the final quilt stitches in Autumn before all the leaves have fallen, or at least before the first snowstorm. When you're finished, hang the piece in the entry to greet your autumn visitors. Then move on to longer autumn and winter projects.

Directions

Finished Size: 37" x 47", with ¼" seams throughout.

Fabric and Other Materials. *Note:* Fabrics should be 44"/45" in cotton or cotton/polyester blends.

Soft brown solid....⅝ yard
 (outer border and one center panel)

Solid peach....⅝ yard
 (middle border and one center panel)

Rust or other dark solid....1 yard
 (one center panel and binding)

Cream solid....1¾ yards
 (inner borders and quilt backing)

¼ yard each of four other colors in a range of golds, tans, browns, or rusts (center panels)

Batting....40" x 50"
 (bonded polyester)

4½ yards of tan double-face ⅛" wide satin ribbon, sewing thread to match fabrics, one spool of natural color quilting thread, scissors, washable marking pencil or soap chips, ruler, cardboard or plastic for quilting templates, sewing machine, pins, thread for basting, frame or hoop for quilting, quilting needles, thimble, iron, and (optional) rotary cutter and mat.

Cutting

Seam allowances are included on all border and panel measurements. However, the measurements do not include enough for mitered corners. Add about 6" to the length of each border measurement if you wish to miter the corners. All borders and panels must be cut on the crosswise of the fabric (there is not enough fabric in the recommended yardages to cut along the lengthwise grain). Cut the following, being sure to cut the borders first.

Cream (inner borders and backing):
   Cut two side borders 2½" x 35½".
   Cut two end borders 2½" x 29½".
   Set remainder aside for the quilt backing.

Peach (middle borders and one center panel):
   Cut two side borders 2½" x 39½".
   Cut two end borders 2½" x 33½".
   Cut one panel 5½" x 25½".

Brown (outer borders and one center panel):
   Cut two side borders 2½" x 43½".
   Cut two end borders 2½" x 37½".
   Cut one panel 5½" x 25½".

Rust (center panel and binding):
   Cut one panel 5½" x 25½".
   Set remainder aside for binding.

From each of the remaining four colors:
   Cut a panel 5½" x 25½" (¼" seam included).

Assembly

Arrange the seven center panels in a layout that balances the value and intensity of the colors. With right sides together, pin and then stitch the long sides of each panel in ¼" seams. Press the seams to one side. Join the borders to the center panels, beginning with the inner cream color border. For each border, attach the sides first, then the ends. See Diagram 1. Press all seams toward the oustide.

Quilting

Make templates of the seven Autumn designs (sheaf of wheat, ear of corn, acorns, oak leaf, apple, jack-o'-lantern, and maple leaf). Divide each center panel into five 5" squares, marking lightly with a washable marker or soap chip. Center the quilting designs in each square and mark lightly around them filling in any details such as the jack-o'-lantern features. Mark five designs on each panel.

Cut a piece of the cream-color fabric about 40" x 50" for the back of the quilt. Place this piece right side down on a flat surface and layer the batting and then the quilt top (right side up) over it. Carefully pin or baste the three layers together.

Using a frame or hoop, quilt the central designs and lines between the designs, along the crosswise seams, and across the three borders as shown in Diagram 2. Diagonal lines are 2½" apart. Remove the bastings.

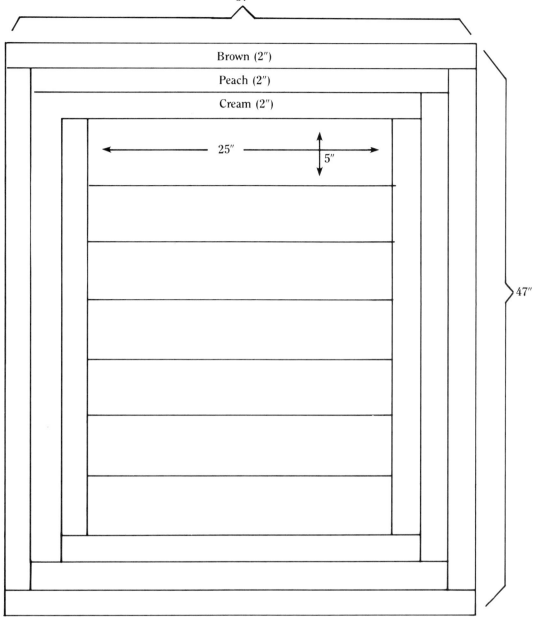

Diagram 1

Finishing

From the remaining rust fabric, cut bias strips 3" wide and piece them to a sufficient length to border the quilt (about 5 yards). Fold the bias in half lengthwise with the wrong sides together. Pin the binding to the quilt top with raw edges flush. Stitch a ¼" seam through all layers. Turn the folded edge of the binding to the quilt back and whipstitch it to the quilt back.

From the ⅛" double-face satin ribbon, cut twenty 7" lengths. Fold them into bows (see Diagram 3) and tack to each of the following quilt designs: sheaf of wheat, acorns, apple, and maple leaf.

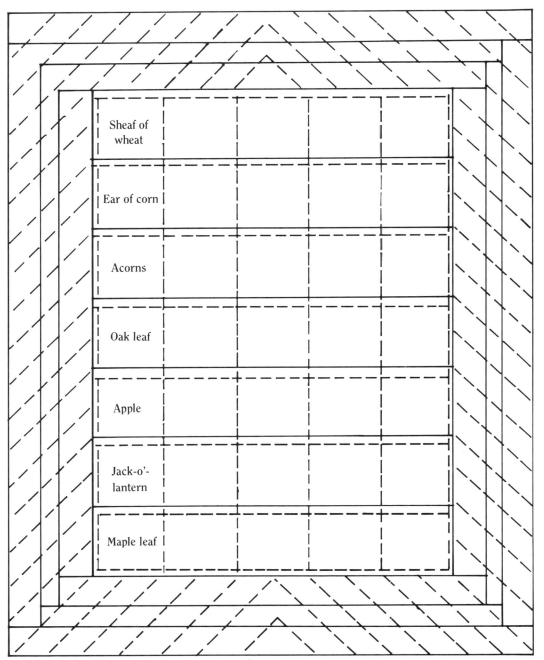

Diagram 2

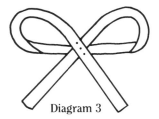

Diagram 3

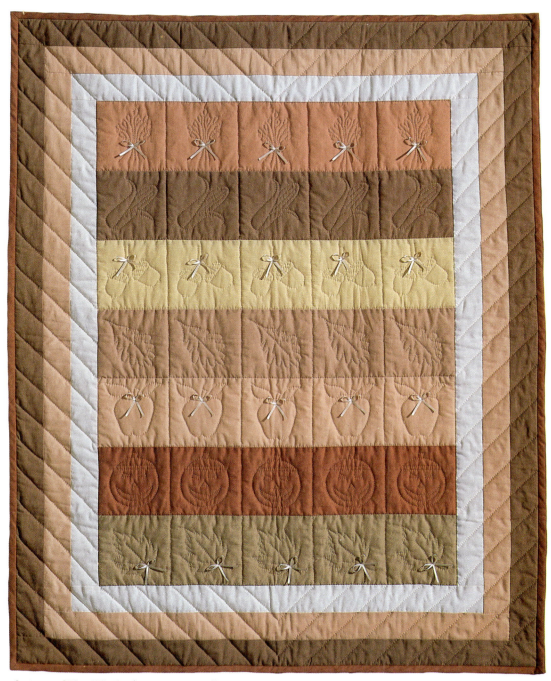

Autumn, 37″ x 47″. For beginners as well as experienced quilters.

Autumn. Detail of quilting designs.

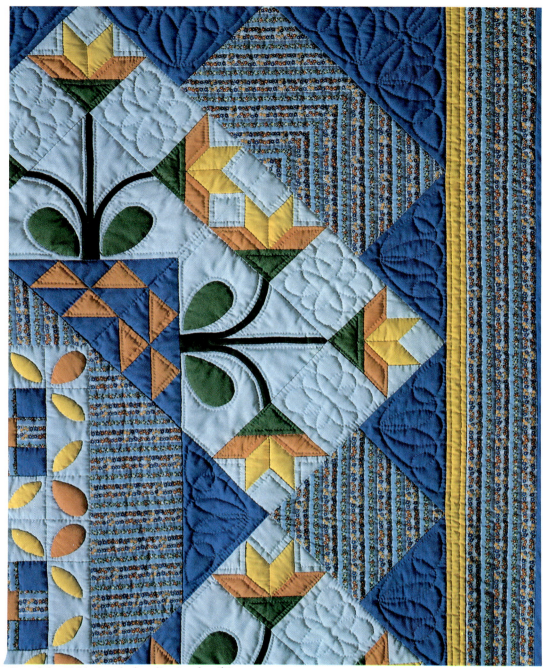
Lilies of the Field. Detail of appliqué and quilting.

Spectrum, 65" x 87½". Different quilting motifs enhance the vibrant rows of color.

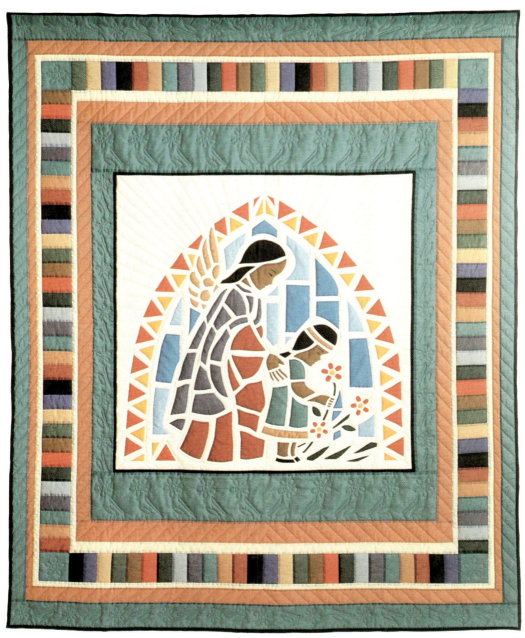

Guardian Angel, 68" x 84". Based on an actual window, the stained glass effect of this quilt is achieved through appliqué.

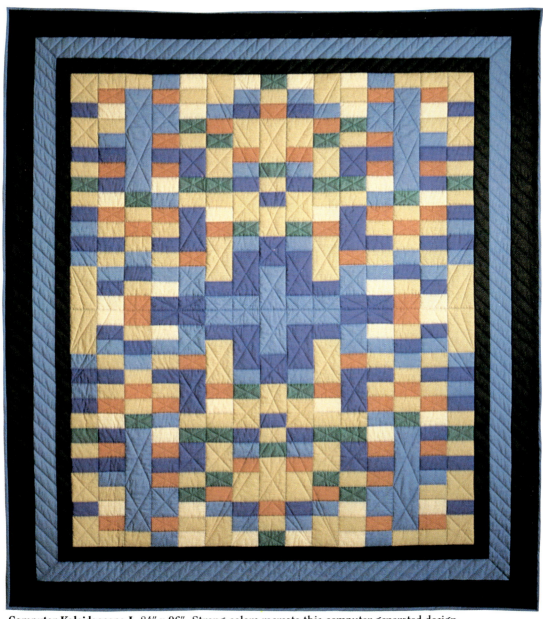
Computer Kaleidoscope I, 84" x 96". Strong colors recreate this computer-generated design.

Computer Kaleidoscope I. Center detail.

Computer Kaleidoscope I. Note varying sizes of rectangles.

Computer Kaleidoscope II, 41″ x 49″. An easy-to-piece design of rectangles.

5

Computer Kaleidoscope II

Computer Kaleidoscope II is a medium-sized project, appropriate for both the beginning and experienced quiltmaker. Measuring 41" x 49", it is suitable for either a wall hanging or a crib quilt. Although I would not consider the pattern difficult, it does require some experience in precision piecing (some of the pieces are as little as 1¼" x 2").

The layout for Computer Kaleidoscope II is based on a graphic design generated on my home computer. As with the other computer quilt in this book, I experimented with colors and rectangular shapes in a graphic kaleidoscope format. Then I wrote and revised a program to employ variables such as the number of colors, the size of the pieces, and the frequency of change in design. I controlled the color, tint, contrast, and brightness with the regular color television hand controls.

From many thousands of possibilities I selected a favorite pattern and adapted it to fabric. In the true spirit of experimentation, I selected fabric colors that are ordinarily not among my personal favorites (you'll have to search hard to find much mauve, lavender, or green in my other quilts). I tried a mixture of solids, a pindot, and a fine print, complemented with a wide border print. You could add your personal touch by increasing the number of print fabrics or reverting to all solid fabrics as in my larger Computer Kaleidoscope quilt.

The inner dark green border gives the effect of the central design flowing into the border at points where the dark green pieces and the dark green border meet. This continuity is further enhanced by quilting lines through the green border and into the small inner pieces, creating secondary quilt designs at the upper and lower borders.

Placement of quilting lines gives a wide latitude for original designs. As the parallel diagonal lines reach another color of fabric, they may change direction, resulting in diamonds, arrows, chevrons, and other unspecified shapes. Let the lines and your imagination flow.

The dimpling effect on the pindot fabric is a result of despair in my attempt to mark and quilt parallel lines true to the dotted lines. The attempt, of course, was futile, as are most attempts to piece and quilt straight lines on pin and micro-dot fabrics. At first I simply left the pindot unquilted, but was not pleased with the visual effect. In order to secure the fabric and give a feeling of "even-quiltedness" throughout, I decided to tack or "dimple" the pindot. I made a diamond-shaped four-point tack on four adjacent dots. Five such dimples are located on each light green piece.

The pleasure in making Computer Kaleidoscope II came mainly in selecting from literally thousands of designs on a video monitor, experimenting with color tones, and placing quilting lines to create unexpected secondary designs. For you, the pleasure may come in the efficiency with which C.K. II can be cut and assembled, the unlimited range of colors and fabrics from which you may choose, or the freedom of not being bound by a traditional block or pattern. All this can be yours, and absolutely no computer knowledge or experience is necessary.

Directions

Finished Size: 41″ x 49″.

Fabric and other Materials:

Note: Fabrics should be 44″/45″ wide in cotton or cotton/polyester blends.

Mauve....¾ yard

Lavender.... 1⅛ yards
 (includes enough for binding)

Dark green solid....1⅝ yards
 (includes inner borders)

Light green pindot....⅝ yard

Print...¾ yard

Border print
 The amount to buy depends on the number of repeats of the border across the fabric width. You need a total of about 5½ yards of a border print that's about 3″ wide. If the border is repeated four times across the width, buy only 1½ yards. If you are buying separate border pieces from a reel or custom cut, buy two pieces, each 1¼ yards long, and two pieces, each 1½ yards long.

Backing....1½ yards
 (good-quality unbleached muslin)

Batting....45″ x 60″
 (bonded polyester)

Sewing thread, one spool of natural color quilting thread, thread for basting, iron, scissors, rust-proof pins, sharp lead pencils, quilting needles, thimble, 18″ or 22″ straightedge, soap chips or washable dressmaker pencils, quilting hoop or frame, and (optional) rotary cutter and mat.

Color Key

M   = Mauve

L   = Lavender

DG   = Dark Green

LG   = Light Green

P   = Print

BP   = Border Print

Cutting and Assembly

Computer Kaleidoscope II is cut and pieced using quick-cutting and machine-piecing techniques. There are no templates. All cutting is done in strips and rows. A rotary cutter and mat are especially appropriate for this pattern. All seams are ¼″ wide. The quilt is assembled in rows, rather than blocks. The top is pieced in quarter-sections that, in turn, are joined to complete the design. Please read all instructions and diagrams before cutting any fabric.

Wash, dry, and press all fabrics. Begin with the mauve (M) fabric (a ¾-yard piece). Fold it into thirds with two lengthwise folds, then pin to secure it. (The tri-folded width will be about 14″ wide, depending on the exact width of your fabric.) With a long straightedge (at least 18″ long) and a soap chip or washable pencil, mark three narrow strips each 1¾″ wide across the folded fabric, as in Diagram 1.* Next, mark two strips 3″ wide on the folded fabric. Last, mark one strip 6¾″ wide, as in the diagram. Note that ¼″ seam allowances are included on all strip measurements.

Note: If you use a straightedge with width markers and a rotary cutter, you may simply cut the strips at the proper intervals and omit the marking step.

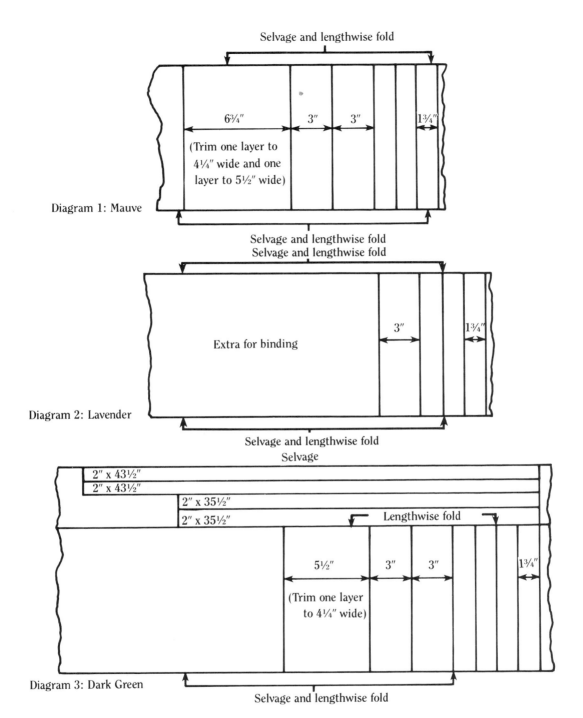

Diagram 1: Mauve

Diagram 2: Lavender

Diagram 3: Dark Green

For the mauve fabric, cut the 1¾" and 3" strips. Then cut along the folds at each end, resulting in nine 1¾" strips and Six 3" strips. Cut the 6¾" strips. Cut along the folds for three separate pieces. Trim one of these to 4¼" wide and the other to 5½" wide.

Proceed with marking and cutting the remaining five fabrics according to Diagrams 2 through 5. Note the following special instructions for each color.

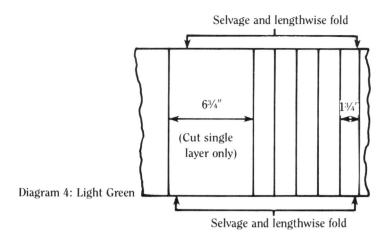

Diagram 4: Light Green

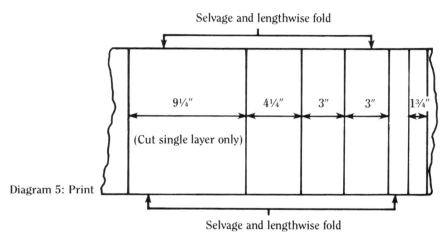

Diagram 5: Print

Lavender: Mark and cut three 1¾" strips; mark and cut one 3" strip.

Dark green: Cut the border pieces first along the length of the fabric (seam allowances included). Cut two side borders 2" x 43½", and cut two end borders 2" x 35½". Then fold the remaining fabric in a lengthwise tri-fold. Mark and cut four 1¾" strips, two 3" strips and one 5½" strip. After cutting along the fold, trim one to 4¼" wide.

Light green: Mark and cut five 1¾" strips, and one 6¾" strip from a single layer of fabric only. To do this, cut along one fold for 6¾" and then along the marked line. (The pattern requires only one light green strip of this size.)

Print: Mark and cut two 1¾" strips, two 3" strips, one 4¼" strip, and mark and cut one 9¼" strip from a single layer of fabric only, as directed for the light green fabric above.

Border print: Cut two side borders 3½" x 49½", and two end borders 3½" x 41½". Seam allowances are included.

Begin with Row 1 and gather the required strips from top to bottom. See Diagrams 6 and 7. Row 1 has a total of seven strips: (L) 3½", (M) 1¾" (LG) 6¾", (L) 1¾", (LG) 3", (M) 1¾", and (DG) 5½". Mark this pile of strips "Row 1" and set it aside. Likewise, gather the strips for the remaining rows and label them.

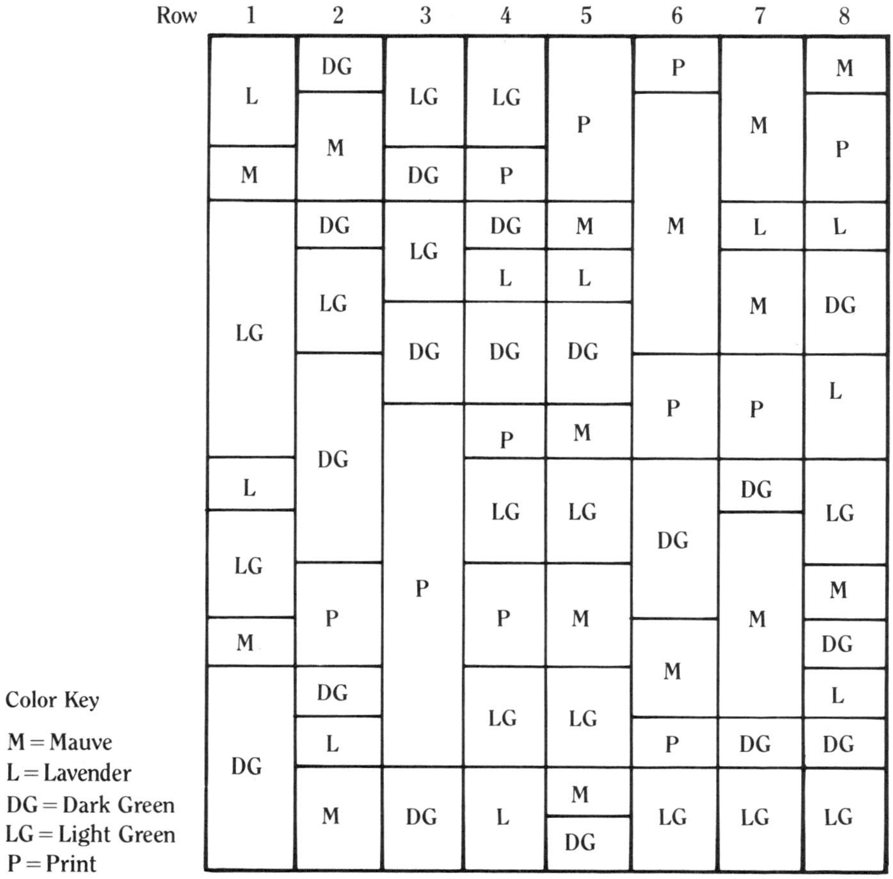

Diagram 6: One-fourth of quilt top

Color Key
M = Mauve
L = Lavender
DG = Dark Green
LG = Light Green
P = Print

Row 1: seven strips
Row 2: nine strips
Row 3: six strips
Row 4: ten strips
Row 5: ten strips
Row 6: seven strips
Row 7: eight strips
Row 8: eleven strips

Gathering and labeling the strips for each row will ensure that you have the correct number and color of strips before proceeding with the assembly. If there is any discrepancy at this point, cut any additional required strips. *Note:* There will be a few extra cut strips to add to your scrap bag.

With right sides together, pin the long sides of the strips of Row 1 according to Diagram 7. One end of each strip should be flush with the end of the next strip. They may be uneven at the other end. Join the strips in ¼" seams. Set Row 1 aside. Likewise, join the strips of the remaining seven rows. Press the seams of all odd-numbered rows up and the even-numbered rows down.

Lay the assembled Row 1 on a flat surface or cutting mat with the wrong sides up. With a straightedge, mark a line along the one side where the edges are flush. Mark four more parallel lines at 2½" intervals, resulting in four columns according to Diagram 8.

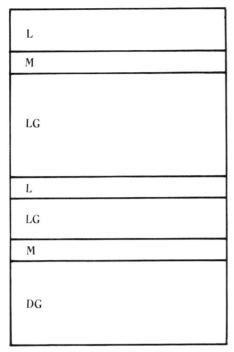

Diagram 7: Row 1

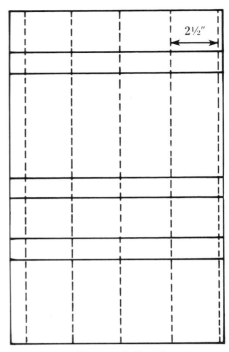

Diagram 8: Row 1

Carefully cut along the marked lines, or mark and cut in one step with a rotary cutter and straightedge. There will be a portion of waste at one side. Label these four strips "Row 1" and set aside. Repeat the marking and cutting for the remaining seven rows.

Assemble one quarter-section of the quilt by joining Row 1 to Row 2, etc., through Row 8, according to Diagram 6. Repeat for another quarter-section.

Join the remaining two quarter-sections in reverse order, Row 8 through Row 1, according to Diagram 9. Press all seams to one side.

Join the four quarter-sections to complete the central design in Diagram 9. *Note:* This is a good point at which to experiment with alternative layouts. Quarter-sections may be placed in any direction and order that you prefer. Diagram 9 illustrates one asymmetrical choice.

Add the borders to the central design. Begin with the 1½" dark green border, then the 3" border print. Miter all corners.

Make a "sandwich" of the backing, batting, and quilt top. Baste or pin the three layers together, working from the center to the outside. Place quilt in a hoop or frame and quilt with natural color thread. Some suggested quilting lines are described below and shown in Diagram 10.

A. Mark and quilt close to the seam around all light green pieces. Make occasional diamond-shaped dimple tracks on the light green pindots (placing dimples on four adjacent pindots).

B. On most of the mauve pieces, mark and quilt diagonal parallel lines about ⅝" apart.

C. On most of the dark green pieces, mark and quilt diagonal parallel lines about ⅝" apart and in the opposite direction of the quilting lines on the mauve fabric.

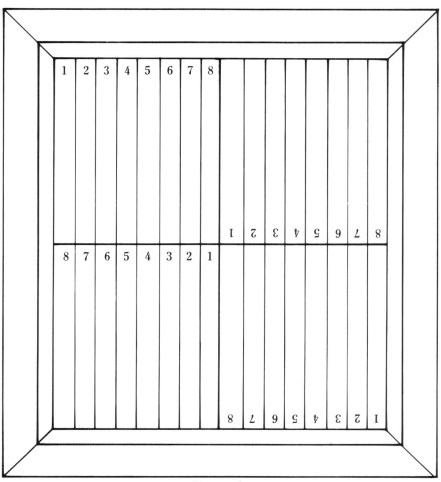

Diagram 9

D. On print fabric pieces, mark and quilt diagonal parallel lines about ⅝″ apart to complete secondary quilted designs on the mauve and dark-green pieces.

E. On lavender pieces, quilt diagonal parallel lines in your choice of directions to complete secondary quilt designs.

F. On the green border, quilt the zigzag designs as illustrated in Diagram 10. On the border print, quilt a cable/parallel line motif (or select a design that best complements your border fabric).

Make bias binding from the remaining lavender fabric and attach it to the quilt.

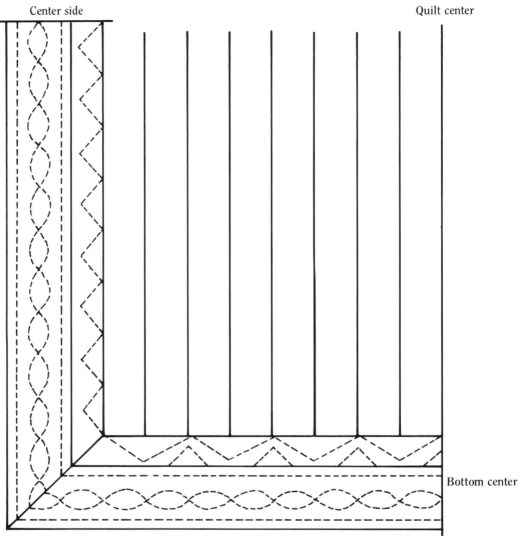

Diagram 10: Suggested border quilting designs

6

Guardian Angel

The Guardian Angel quilt is one of our family's favorites. The central design is based on a cut-glass window at the St. Francis Solanus Mission in Reserve, Wisconsin. We like to visit there as a family and were immediately taken when we saw the stained-glass window. The simplicity and warmth of the message is powerful. The angel and child personify the tenderness and caring we long to express.

I took a photograph of the window when I first saw it. I thought about it frequently, gazing at the snapshot from time to time for several years before I finally became inspired to try the work in fabric. Guardian Angel is dedicated to my son Matthew, a member of the Oneida Tribe of Wisconsin Indians.

Guardian Angel is probably most accurately described as an adaptation of a design. The central appliqué is a reproduction of the actual window. I have tried to duplicate the sizes, shapes, and rich colors as they really exist. Beyond the appliqué center is a medallion layout of eight borders designed to make the work suitable for either wall or bed. In order to increase the quilt length, border widths vary on the sides and ends. Because of the variation between the side and end borders, most corners cannot be mitered.

Multiple narrow borders and the sheer number of appliqué pieces (106 different shapes and more than 160 pieces to appliqué) may sound discouraging. An easier option is to make a smaller wall hanging of the appliquéd area only, with one or two borders to frame it. You might also use the child and flowers alone for a rectangular banner or hanging. Either choice would still convey the tender mood portrayed by the actual window.

My personal fabric selection was solid colors only, as these best reflected the tone and texture of the glass. Only solid colors were used in the borders, as well. The darkest color, black, appears in the hair of the angel and child, in the narrow border next to the appliqué, and in the binding. Other border colors (teal, spice, and muslin) were taken from colors within the appliquéd portion and repeated. The teal and spice borders are the only ones wide enough to accommodate the quilted floral motif. Parallel diagonal lines of quilting are used on the remaining borders.

To minimize distraction from the angel and child, the center is only modestly quilted. There is no quilting on the appliques themselves. Instead, I have stitched double outlines around most of the pieces. Occasional lines to emphasize shapes such as the child's garment, the angel's gown and robe, and the child's feet and head were added later. The radiating lines in the outer area of the muslin background complete the center quilting.

My favorite method for precision hand-appliqué of 100 percent cotton fabrics includes the use of a pressing template for each shape. Make a template (without seam allowances) from lightweight cardboard, such as a manila file folder. Place the template on the wrong side of the fabric piece, which has been cut to include seam allowances of between ⅛" and ¼". Next, press the seams up and around the cardboard piece, using a generous portion of steam to set the edges. Baste all the edges under, or immediately place and pin the pieces onto the background.

Begin appliquéing, using thread that matches the color of the fabric piece and tiny, snug stitches that fall between the appliqués and the background. When completed, good hand appliqué should hardly be distinguishable from good piecing.

If you're in a hurry, don't attempt to make the Guardian Angel. However, if you are looking for a pleasurable experience in solid-color fabrics and appliqué, this is the pattern for you. The rewards will come not only in the finished quilt, but from a well-earned feeling of accomplishment and the warmth of the Guardian Angel's message.

Directions

Finished Size: 63" x 84".

Fabric and Other Materials. *Note:* Fabrics should be 44"/45" wide in 100 percent cotton.

Black....2 yards

Teal....2½ yards

Spice....2¼ yards

Blue/Gray....½ yard

Brown....½ yard

Light blue....¼ yard

Medium blue....½ yard

Cranberry....½ yard

Green....¼ yard

Gold....¼ yard

Orange-red....½ yard

Red....¼ yard

Yellow....¼ yard

Backing....6½ yards
(good-quality unbleached muslin.) Set aside a 5-yard piece for borders and backing. Set aside a 1½-yard piece for the background of the center appliqued portion of the quilt.

Batting....72" x 90"
(bonded polyester)

Thread for piecing, thread in several colors for appliqué, natural color quilting thread for hand-quilting, black embroidery thread, and the usual sewing and quilting tools.

Cutting and Assembly

Carefully read through all directions before cutting any fabric. Pattern pieces are coded GA for Guardian Angel, followed by a letter that refers to the fabric color.

Color Key

B = Black
T = Teal
S = Spice
BG = Blue/Gray
BR = Brown
LB = Light Blue
MB = Medium Blue
C = Cranberry
G = Green
GO = Gold
OR = Orange/Red
R = Red
Y = Yellow

Make templates for all pattern pieces. Most templates will be used to cut only one fabric piece. Eight templates, including some orange and yellow triangles and the flower centers and petals, will require multiple cuttings. The number of pieces to cut is designated on these patterns and should be noted on the template.

The center features thirteen different colors against a muslin background. The total number of appliqué pieces to cut by color is as follows:

B — seven
T — three
S — two
BG — sixteen
BR — sixteen
LB — nine
MB — ten
C — nine
G — eleven
GO — eleven
OR — twenty-five
R — fifteen
Y — twenty-eight

Total: 162 pieces

Add a ¼" seam allowance to all appliqué pieces. Turn under all edges and baste or press. Prepare the 1½-yard muslin background piece by cutting it down to a 40½" square (seams included). Then place the appliqué pieces on the background according to Diagram 1. See Diagram 2 for detail on the child and flowers. On the two sides and bottom of the design, leave a small clearance (about 1½") between the appliqué pieces and the raw edge of the muslin. Leave a greater clearance (about 3") at the top. Pin or baste the pieces in place, then appliqué it with a blind stitch, using matching thread for each color piece. Use black embroidery thread to stitch the eye and eyebrow detail using a chain or satin stitch.

Diagram 1

There is a total of eight borders. See Diagram 3. They are numbered, reading from the center out, beginning with the narrow black border around the appliqué. Cut borders according to the following chart (¼" seam allowances are included in these measurements).

Border #1 (black): Cut two sides 1" x 40".
Cut two ends 1" x 41".

Border #2 (teal): Cut two sides 3¼" x 41½".
Cut two ends 7½" x 47".

Border #3 (spice): Cut two sides 2½" x 55½".
Cut two ends 3½" x 51".

Border #4 (muslin): Cut two sides 1¼" x 61½". Cut two ends 2 x 52½".

Border #5 (pieced) From all other colors, except light blue, yellow, muslin and teal, cut twelve rectangles from Border pattern #1.
(Note that a ¼" seam allowance must be added to the rectangles.) This will give you 120 rectangles (ten colors times twelve pieces each). Join thirty-two rectangles in an orderly repeated color fashion for each side. Join twenty-six rectangles each for the top and bottom. You will have four pieces left over to add to your scrap bag.

Diagram 2

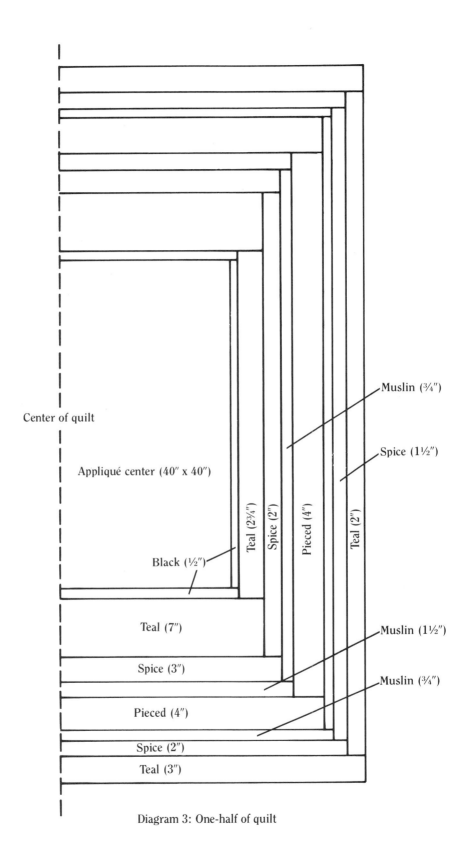

Diagram 3: One-half of quilt

(Teal) Cut four squares from border pattern #2. (Note: ¼" seams must be added to these squares.) Add one square to each end of these top and bottom pieced borders.

Border #6 (muslin): Cut two sides 1¼" x 72½" Cut two ends 1¼" x 62".

Border #7 (spice): Cut two sides 2" x 73½". Cut two ends 2½" x 65".

Border #8 (teal): Cut two sides 2½" x 78½". Cut two ends 3½" x 68½".

Attach Border #1 to the appliquéd center panel. Add the sides first, then the top and bottom. Continue adding Borders #2 through #8 in the same fashion (sides first, then ends). Use Diagram 3 as your guide. It will not be possible to miter the corners due to variations in the widths of the crosswise and lengthwise borders.

Quilting

Cut the 5-yard muslin piece into two 2½ yard pieces. From one piece, cut two panels 15" wide and 2½ yards long. Join these to the sides of the other uncut piece. Assemble the three layers of the back, batting, and quilt top. Pin or baste together.

Mark the floral quilting designs in the inner teal borders (Border #2) and the outer teal end borders (Border #8). Quilt around all appliqué pieces. Quilt radiating lines on the center muslin background. Quilt diagonal lines on the spice borders (Borders #3 and #7) and the outer teal side borders (Border #8). Quilt a flower in each corner square of Border #5. Quilt close to the seam around each rectangle in Border #5. Quilt along all borders close to the seams.

Bind with continuous bias binding made from the remaining black fabric.

Appendix A
How to Make Narrow Bias Strips for Appliqué

Much of the anxiety that some quilters associate with appliqué comes from the frustration of trying to accurately turn under and apply narrow strips for stems, vines, handles, etc. The description and diagrams that follow show a method that is efficient and results in greater accuracy. This method is suitable for any pattern where narrow bias strips are needed, such as flowers, stems, vines, branches, wreaths, garlands, basket handles, Celtic work, and stained glass appliqué.

1. For finished ¼" wide strips, cut a fabric strip of true bias that is ⅞" wide and the desired length. See Figure 1.

Note: To determine the width to cut the fabric strips, multiply the desired finished width by two and add ⅜". Cut bias strips of this width. For example, to make ½" wide strips, cut bias strips 1⅜" wide (½" x 2 + ⅜" = 1⅜").

2. Fold the fabric strip in half lengthwise with wrong sides together and the raw edges flush. Seam together in a ⅛" seam, as in Figure 2.

3. Make a ¼" wide strip of lightweight cardboard or metal (not plastic), or use a commercial "bias bar." Be sure that the substance selected is heat-resistant and free of

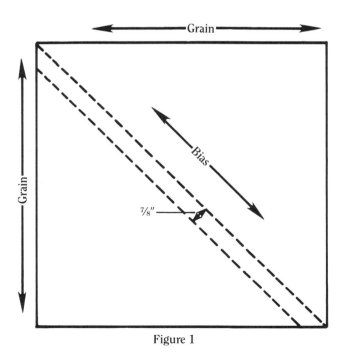

Figure 1

Figure 2

sharp edges. Insert the strip inside the bias fabric tube and center the seam and raw edges along one side of the strip. See Figures 3 and 4.

4. Steam-press the strip on the seam side first. Then press the right side of the bias strip.

5. Remove the cardboard (or metal) strip. The bias is ready to be applied.

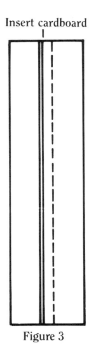

Figure 3

Figure 4

Appendix B
More Ideas for Creating Your Own Quilting Designs

In the following examples, I have listed and diagrammed guidelines for making original quilting designs. These steps are easy to follow, using a simple design motif. The designs are not difficult. I have used procedures similar to these to make many quilting designs. For instance, the quilting designs for Lilies of the Field are based on a simple teardrop motif arranged to fit various shaped background and border areas.

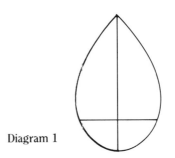

Diagram 1

Several of the Lilies of the Field designs are outlined below. Read through the examples step by step. Then begin with a clean piece of paper and try your own designs. The small triangle and square designs are given here. The larger triangular quilting design for Lilies is made with the same teardrop shapes. After you have tried these examples, locate the larger design and see if you can analyze how it is made. Then try your own. The possibilities are infinite.

Design A is for the background square area between the flowers of the North Carolina Lily block.

1. Make a cardboard or plastic template of the teardrop shape (body piece of the honeybee). Draw a line down the center, and a line perpendicular to it ½" from the curved end. See Diagram 1.

2. Make a 4¼" square of paper. With a pencil, lightly mark the four quarter grid lines and the two diagonal lines. See Diagram 2. Draw a teardrop shape in each quarter.

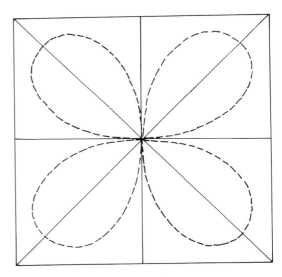

Diagram 2

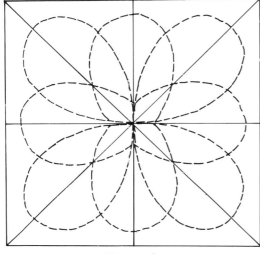

Diagram 3

3. Place the template toward the four sides, with the rounded end about ¼″ from the edge of the paper, as in Diagram 3. Trace around the template, stopping at the center grid lines on each side.

4. Selectively erase the inner lines to reveal the central floral shape, as in Diagram 4. Then erase all the grid lines.

Design B is an alternative design for the same background square area.

1 and 2: These steps are the same as in the previous example, with one exception: Place the rounded end at the center and draw the teardrop shape in each corner, as in Diagram 5.

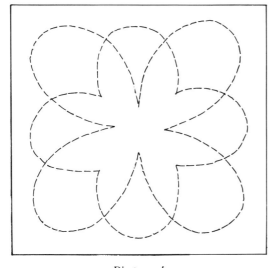

Diagram 4
Design A

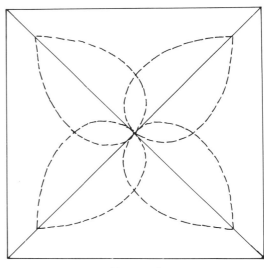

Diagram 5

3. Place the template toward the four sides, with the pointed end about ¼" from the edge of the paper, as in Diagram 6. Trace around the template, stopping at the center grid lines on each side.

4. Selectively erase inner lines to reveal the finished design, as in Diagram 7. Then erase the grid lines.

Design C is for the dark blue triangles on the Lilies quilt. This design uses two shapes: the small teardrop template from the previous examples and another larger teardrop template as in Diagram 8 (the leaf from the North Carolina Lily pattern).

1. Make the larger template and draw in the center line.

2. On white paper, make a right triangle that is 6⅜" on the two short sides and 9" on the long side. With a pencil, lightly mark in a ¼" clearance on all three sides and a grid line that divides it into two parts. See Diagram 9.

3. With the large template, draw a teardrop in the center of the triangle (Diagram 9). Then trace another shape on either side, with the tips meeting at the same point and the edges along the clearance lines on the sides. See Diagram 10.

4. Next, add a small teardrop shape in the two corners, being sure to clear the edges. See Diagram 11.

5. Erase grid and clearance lines.

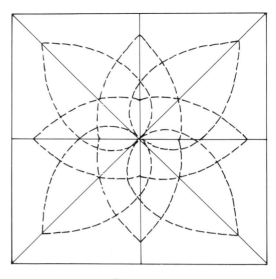

Diagram 6

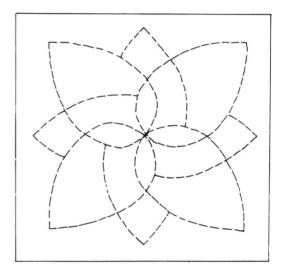

Diagram 7
Design B

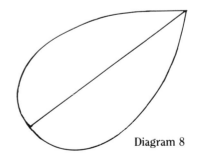

Diagram 8

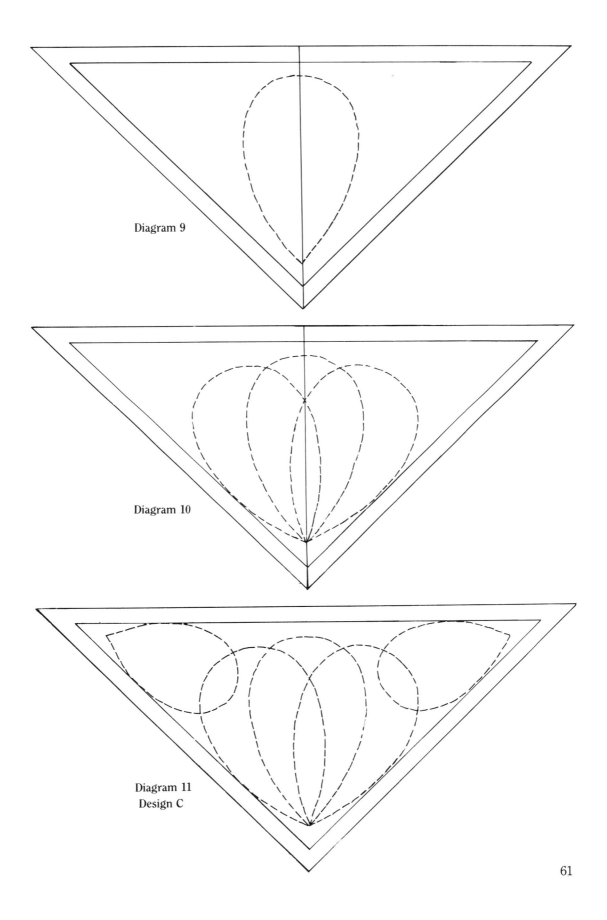

Diagram 9

Diagram 10

Diagram 11
Design C

Bibliography

For Instructional Basics and Beyond

Beyer, Jinny. *The Art and Technique of Creating Medallion Quilts*. McLean, Va.: EPM Publications, Inc., 1982.

Fine Patchwork and Quilting. Tokyo, Japan: Ondorisha Publishers, Ltd., 1983.

Florence, Judy. *Award-Winning Quilts and How to Make Them*. Lombard, Ill.: Wallace-Homestead Book Co., 1986.

Hinson, Dolores A. *Quilting Manual*. New York: Hearthside Press, Inc., 1970.

Martin, Judy. *Patchworkbook* (Easy Lessons for Quilt Design & Construction). New York: Charles Scribner's Sons, 1983.

Quilting (Patchwork & Appliqué). Menlo Park, Calif.: Lane Publishing Co., 1982.

For Pattern Ideas and Inspiration

Hornung, Clarence P. *Handbook of Designs and Devices*. New York: Dover Publications, Inc., 1959.

Malone, Maggie. *1001 Patchwork Designs*. New York: Sterling Publishing Co., Inc., 1982.

Nelson, Cyril I. *The Quilt Engagement Calendars*. New York: E. P. Dutton, Inc., 1974 to date.

Nelson, Cyril I., and Carter Houck. *Treasury of American Quilts*. New York: Crown Publishers Inc., 1982.

Pottinger, David. *Quilts from the Indiana Amish*. New York: E. P. Dutton, Inc., 1983.

About the Author

Award-Winning Quilts, Book II is Judy Florence's second book about quiltmaking. Her first book, titled *Award-Winning Quilts and How to Make Them* is currently available from Wallace-Homestead Book Company.

Judy's quilts have been featured in several periodicals and calendars, including *Quilt Art '85* and the fifteenth anniversary issue of *Quilter's Newsletter Magazine*. Her quilts have won many awards, and, as a result, she has been invited to conduct workshops throughout the United States and Canada.

Judy's other favorite pastime is her family. She and her husband have two sons — one from the Oneida Tribe of Wisconsin Indians, the other from Korea. Interests in English as a second language, cross-cultural study, and bi-racial family issues occupy much of the family's time. All four enjoy travel and a variety of ethnic and international events.

The Florences live in Eau Claire, Wisconsin.

Judy Florence (pictured at left).

Templates

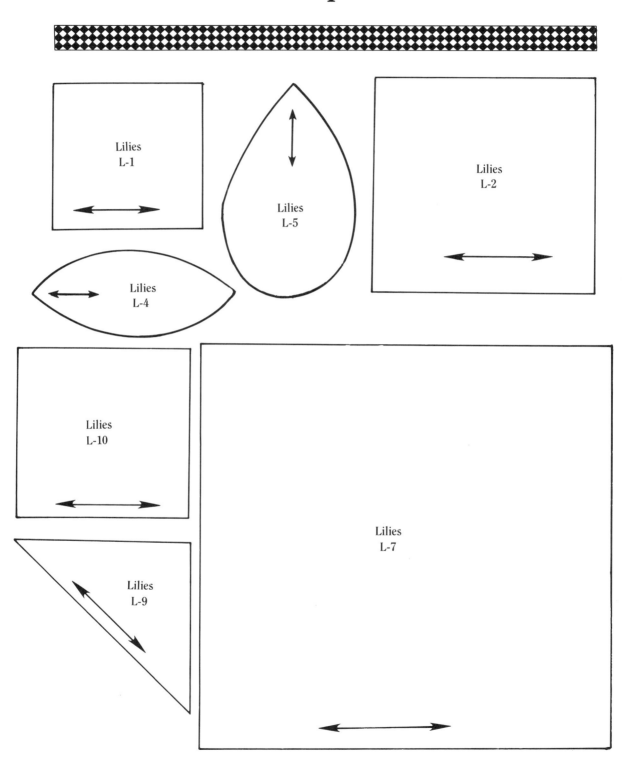

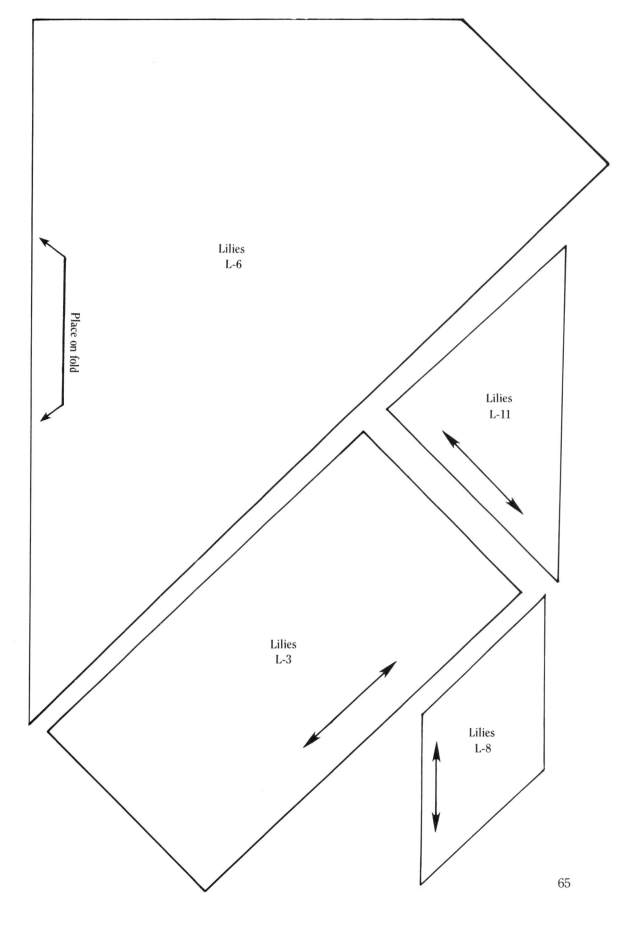

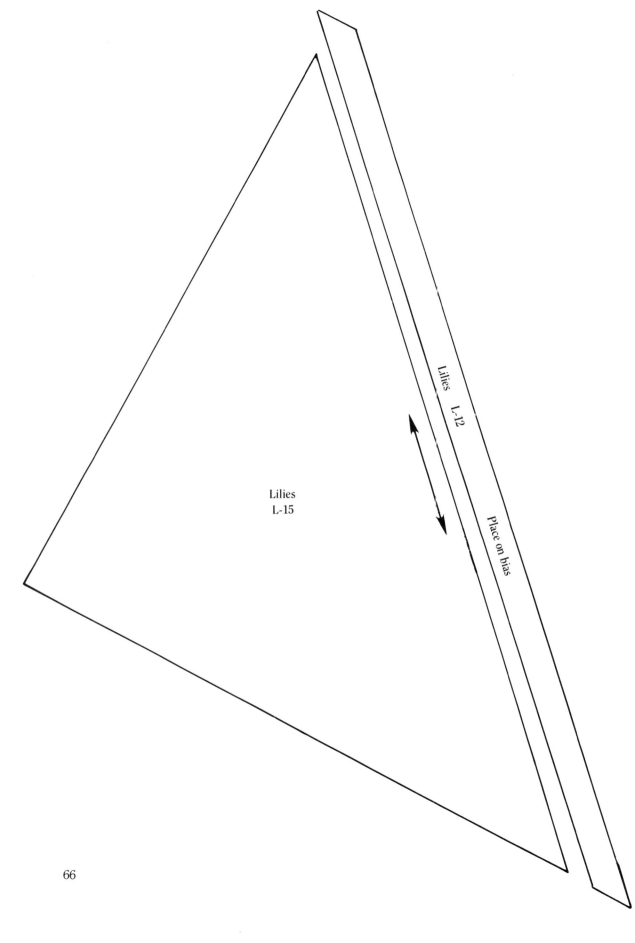

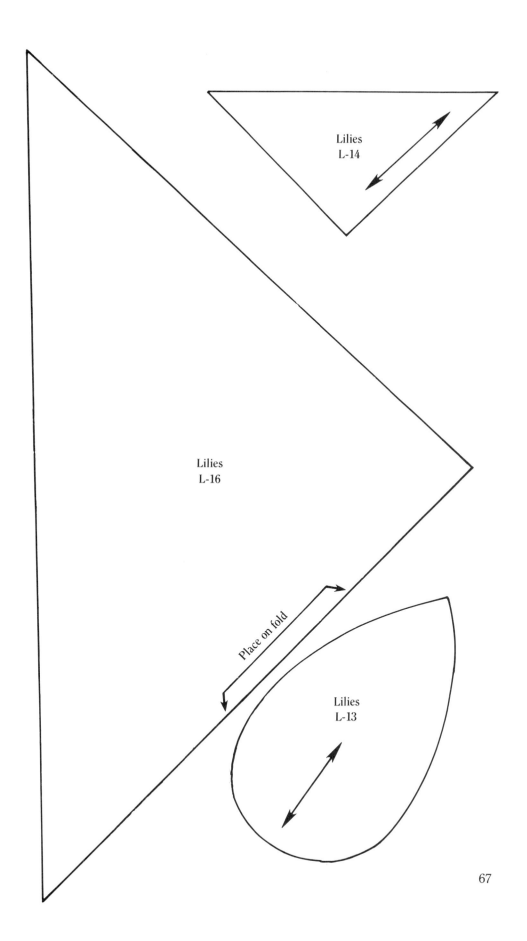

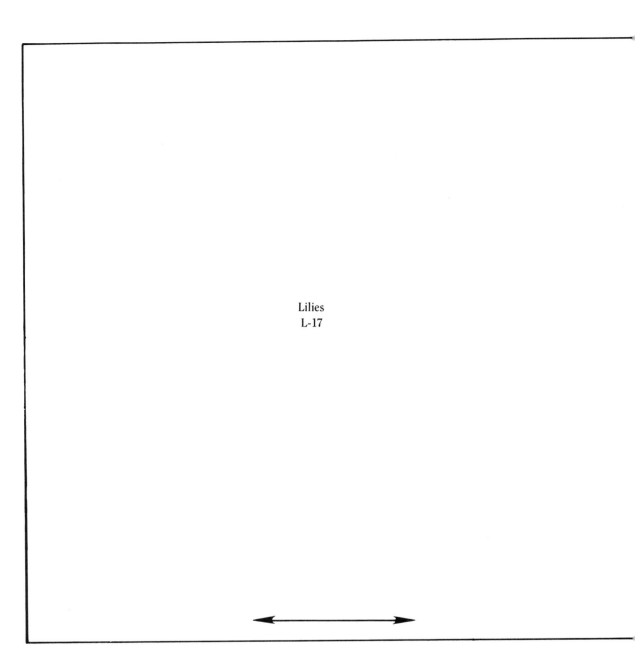

Lilies
L-17

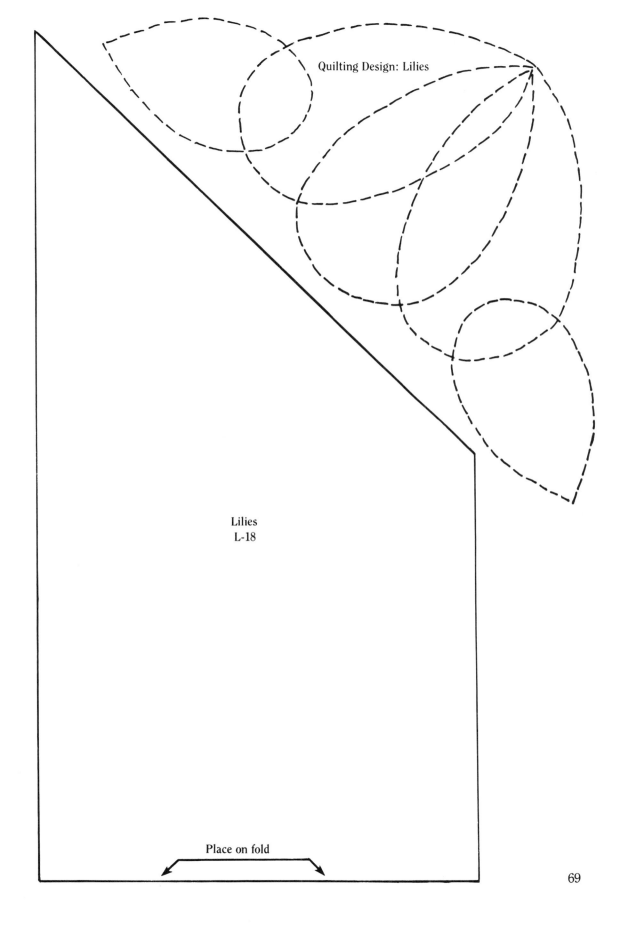

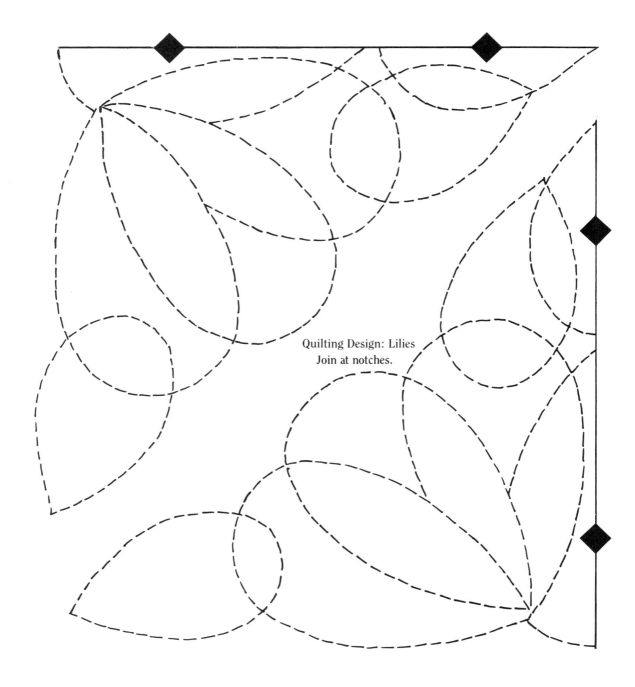

Quilting Design: Lilies
Join at notches.

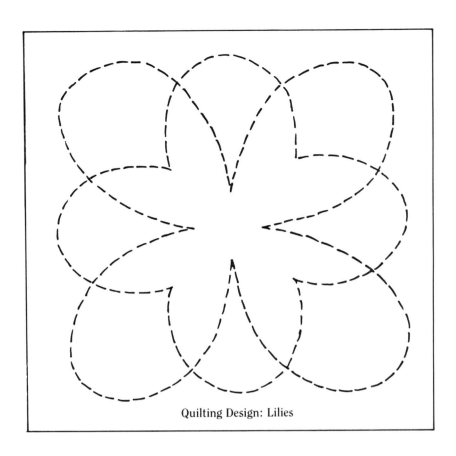
Quilting Design: Lilies

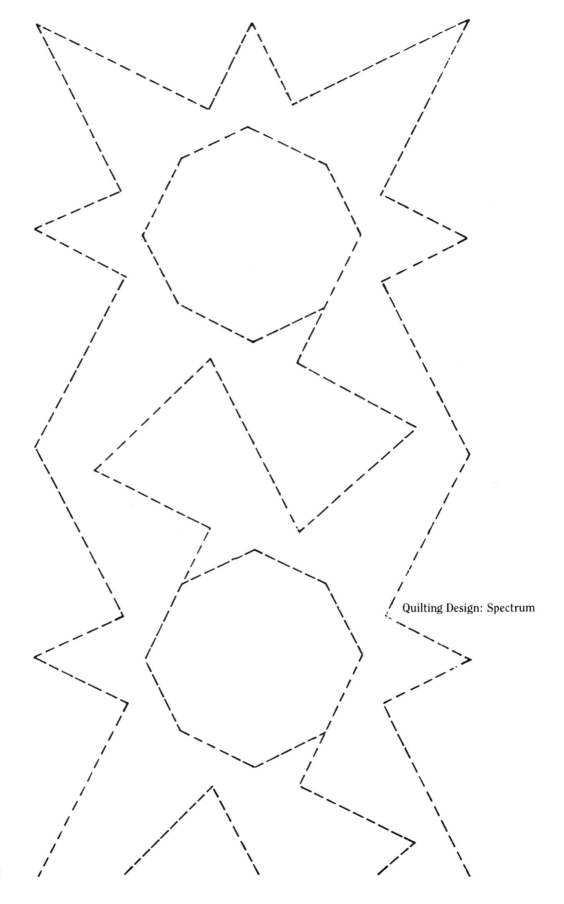

Quilting Design: Spectrum

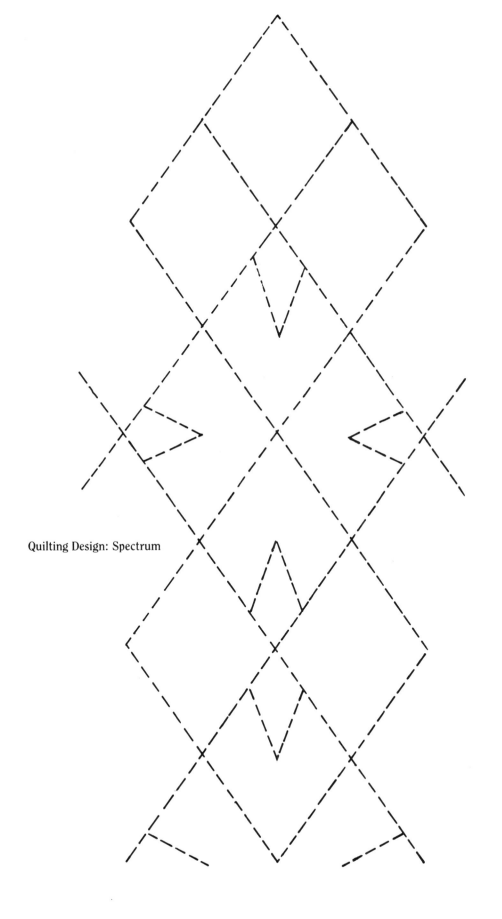

Quilting Design: Spectrum

Quilting Design: Spectrum

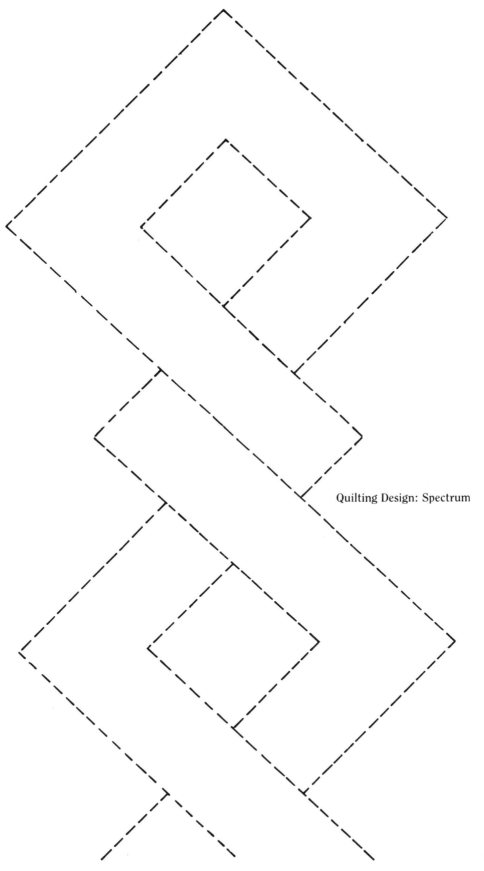

Quilting Design: Spectrum

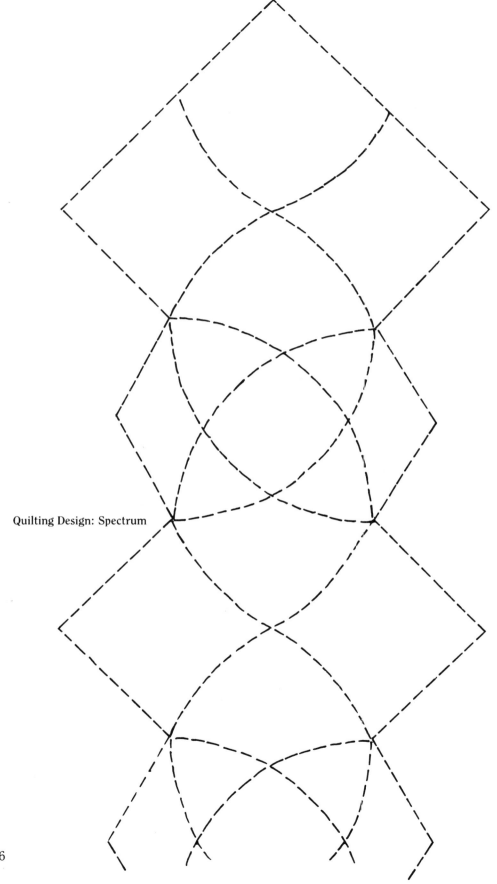

Quilting Design: Spectrum

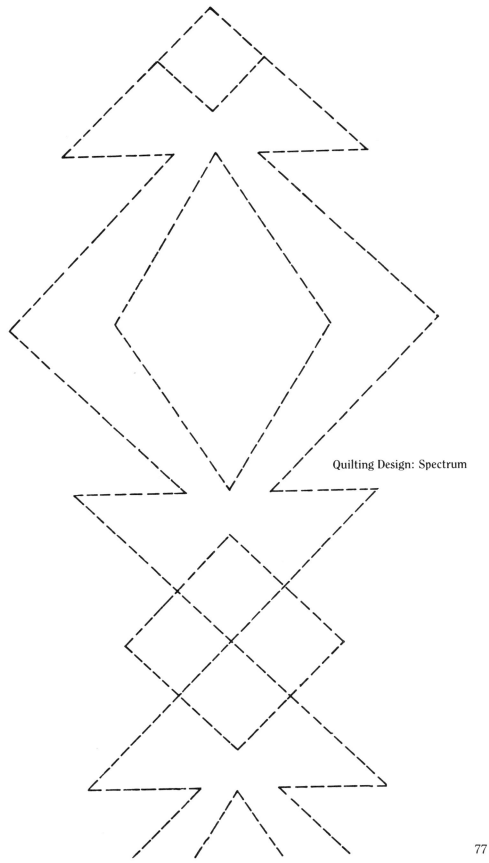

Quilting Design: Spectrum

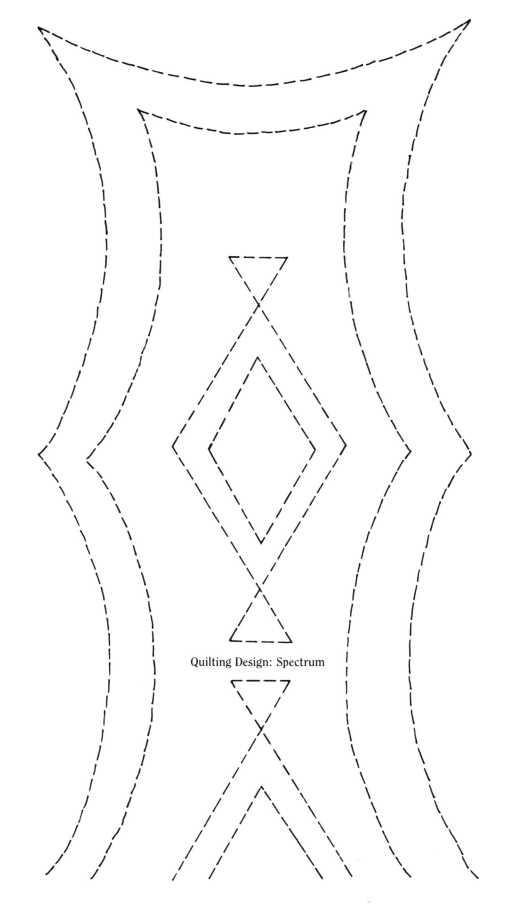

Quilting Design: Spectrum

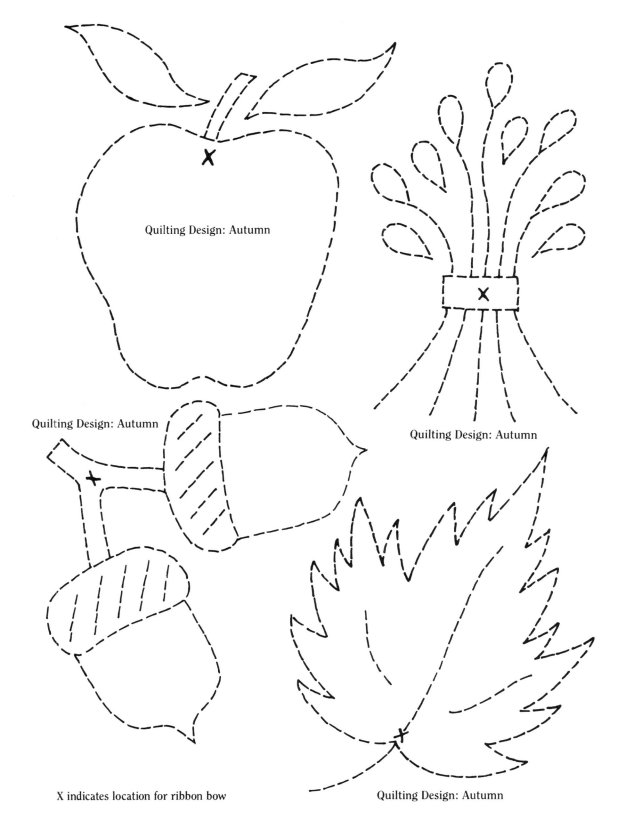

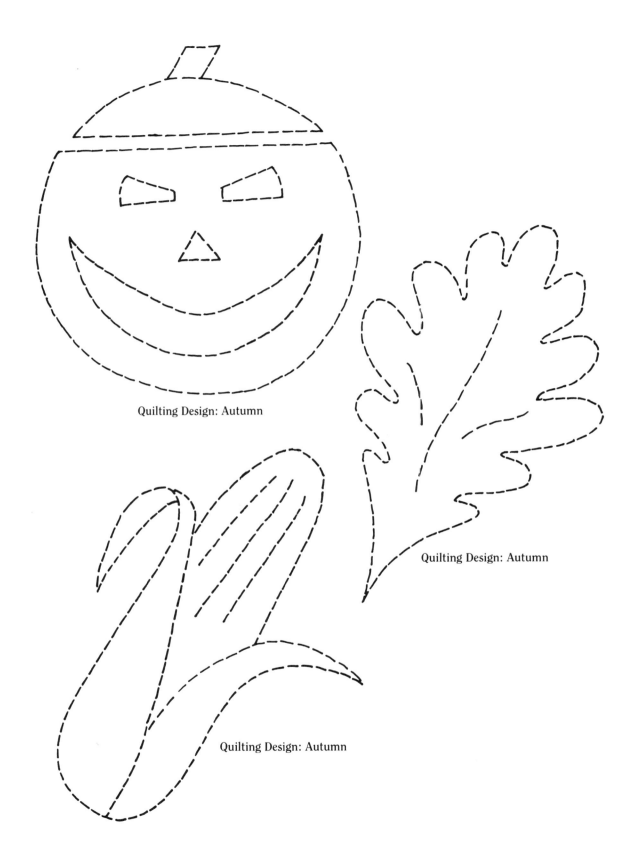

Quilting Design: Autumn

Quilting Design: Autumn

Quilting Design: Autumn

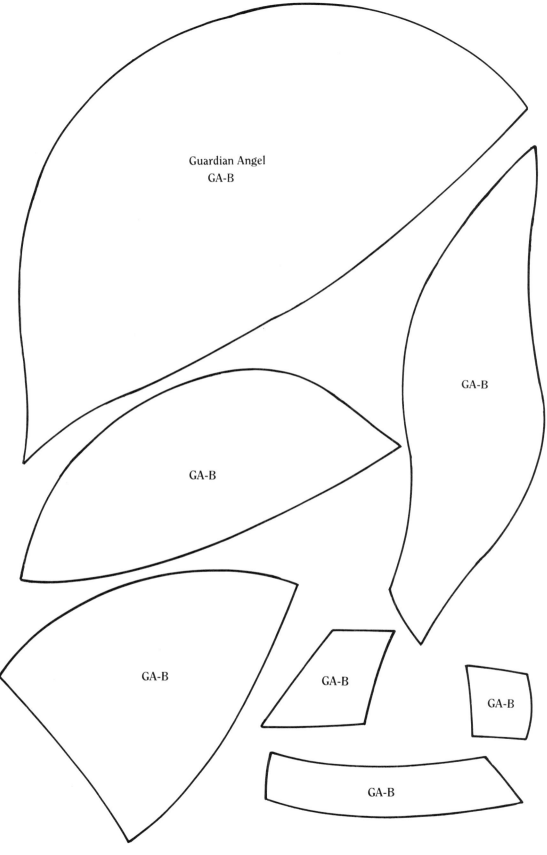

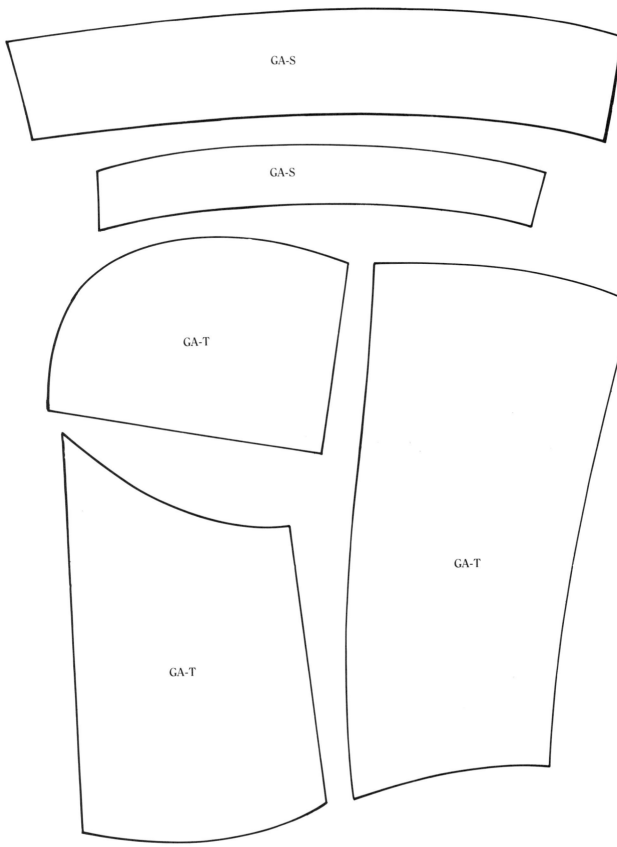

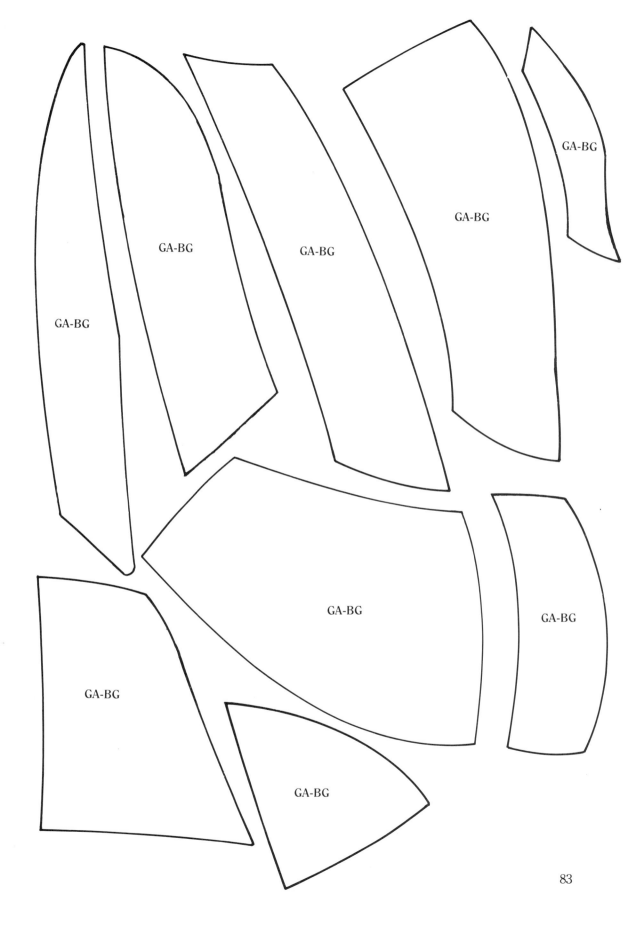

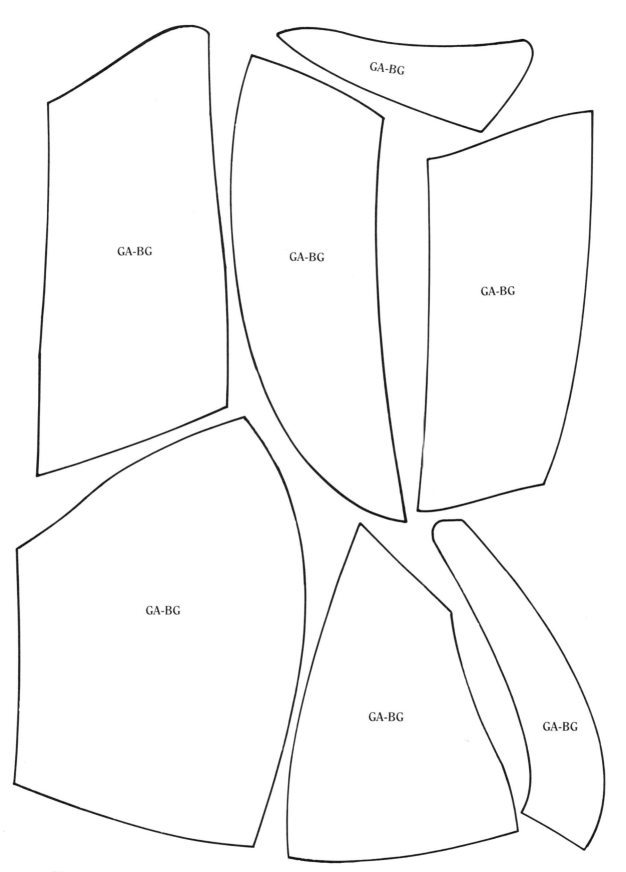

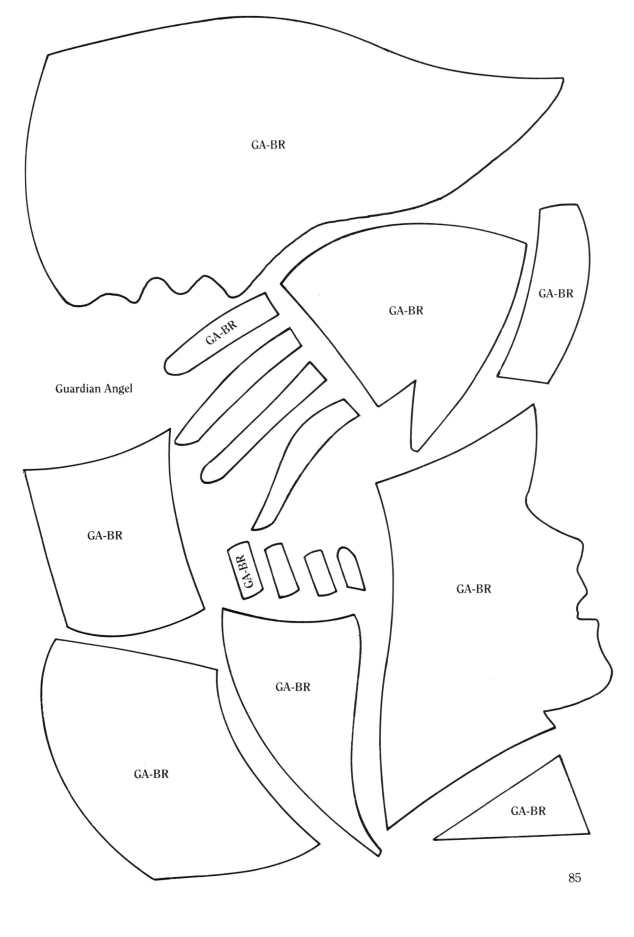

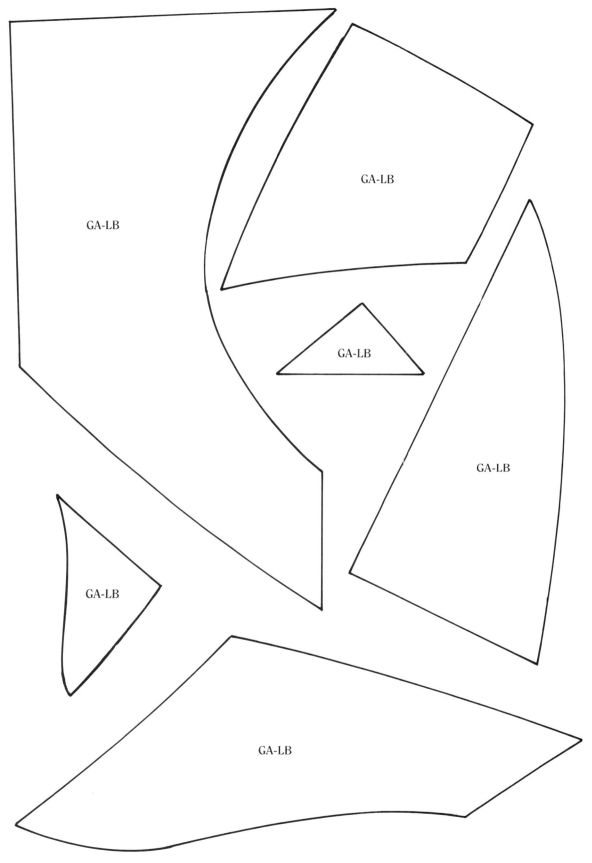

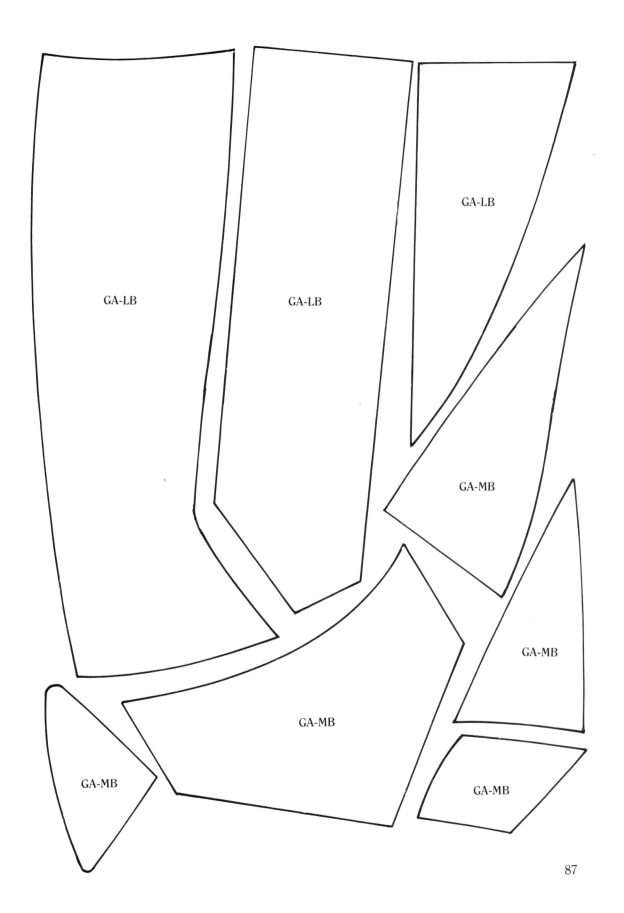

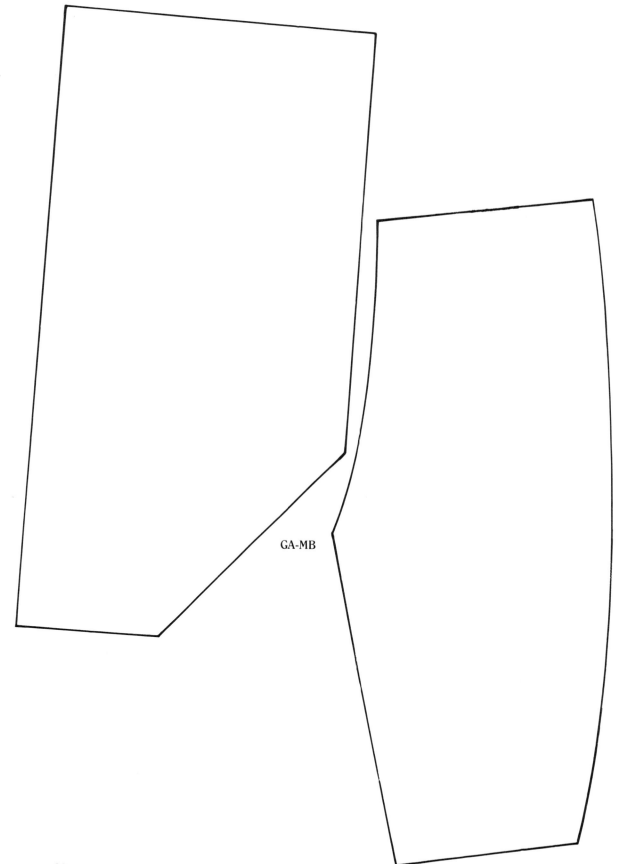

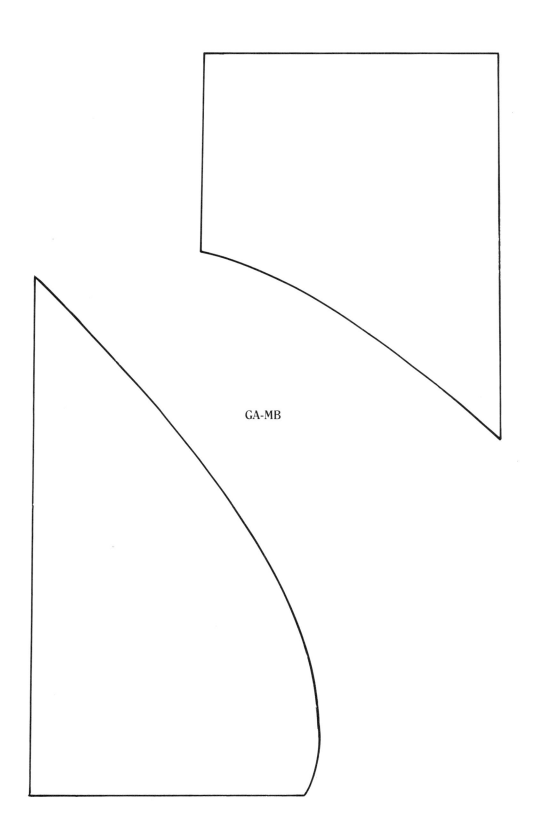

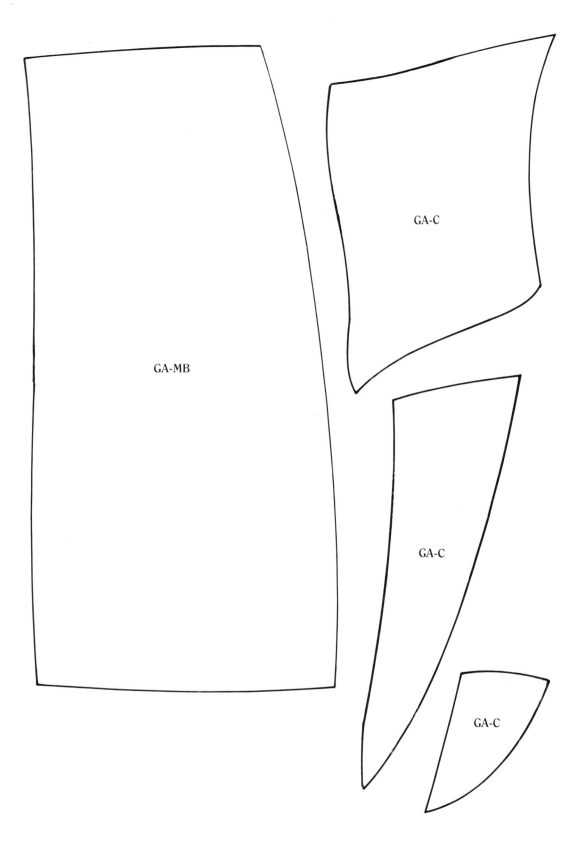

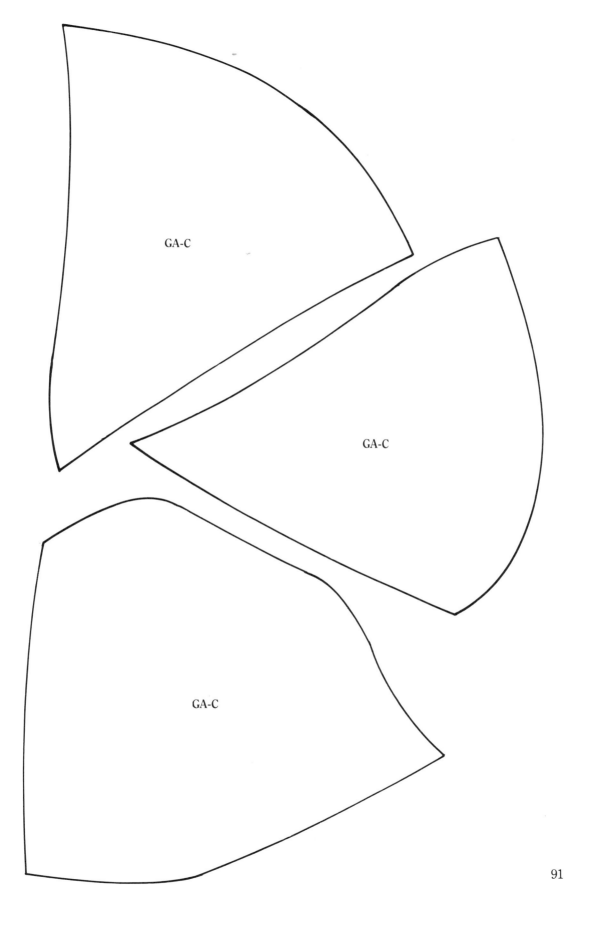

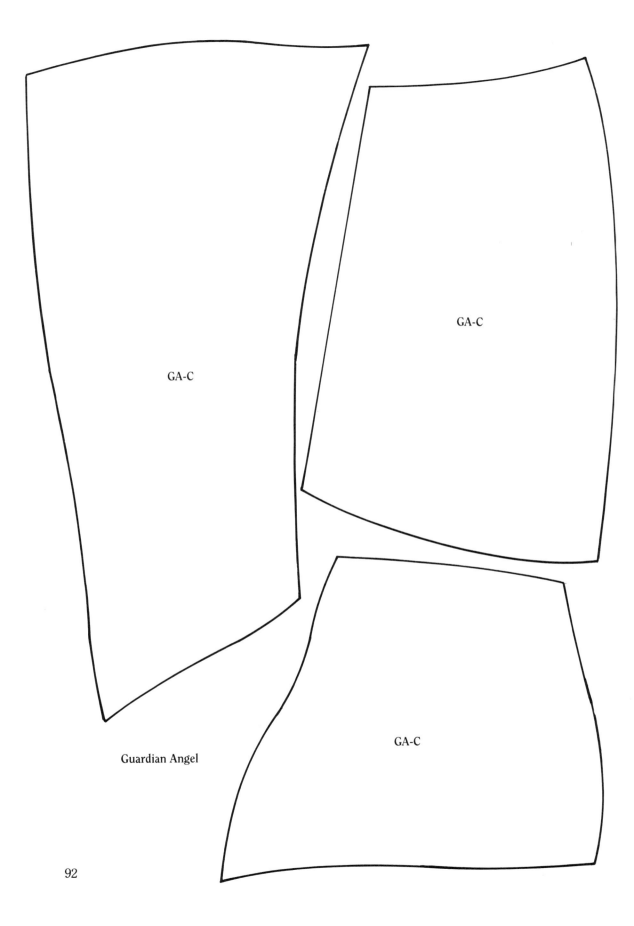

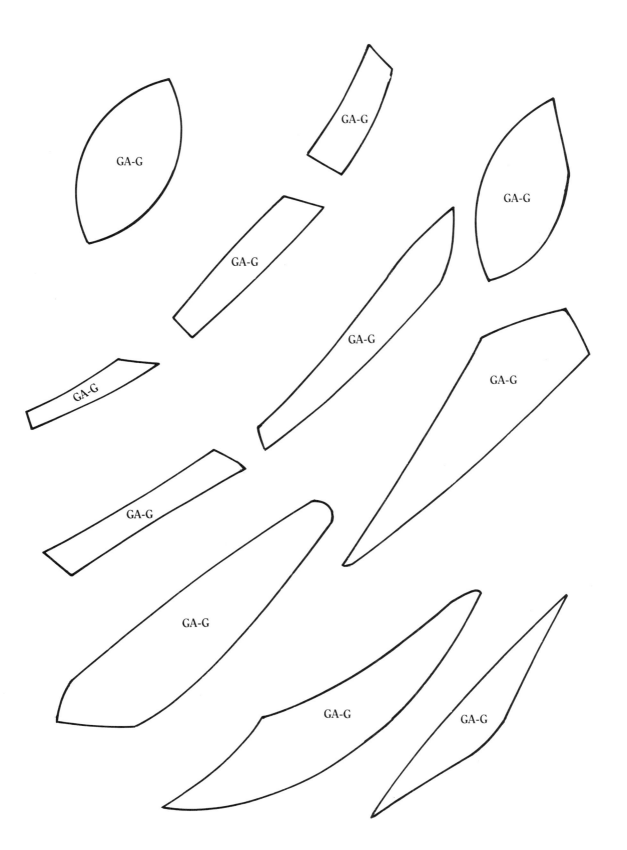

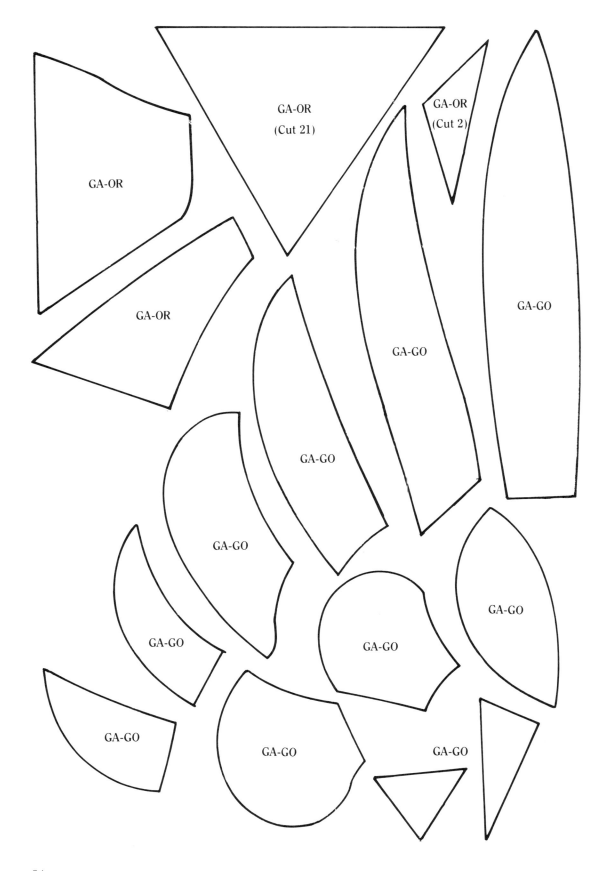

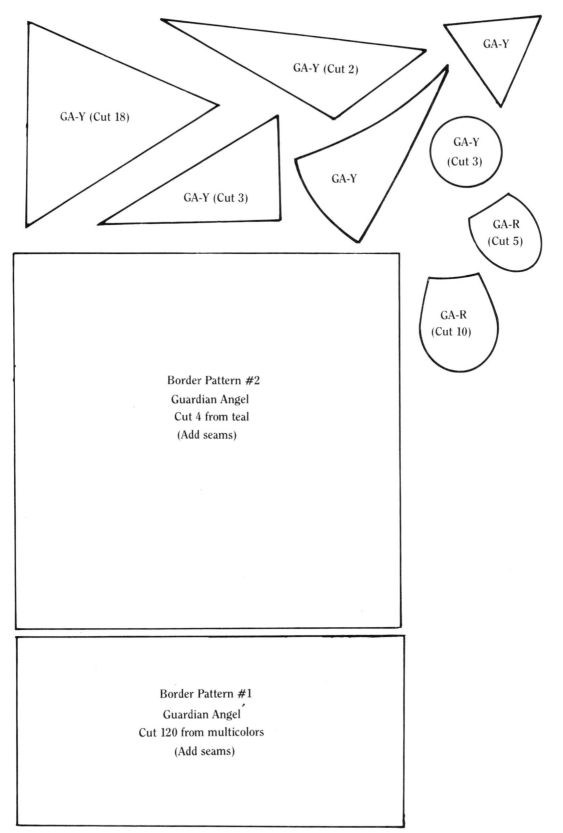

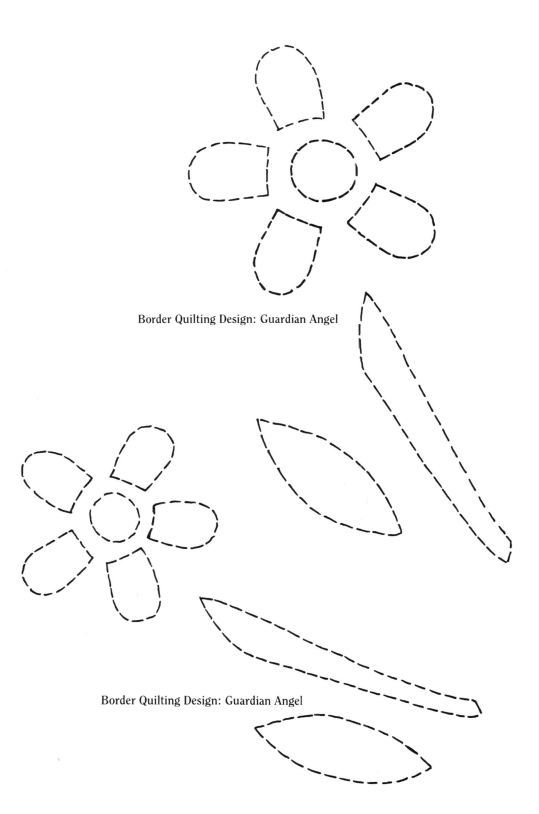

Border Quilting Design: Guardian Angel

Border Quilting Design: Guardian Angel